NO PLACE FOR THE WEAK

A TRUE STORY OF DEVIANCE, TORTURE AND SOCIAL CLEANSING

RYAN GREEN

For Helen, Harvey, Frankie and Dougie

Disclaimer

This book is about real people committing real crimes. The story has been constructed by facts but some of the scenes, dialogue and characters have been fictionalised.

Polite Note to the Reader

This book is written in British English except where fidelity to other languages or accents are appropriate. Some words and phrases may differ from US English.

ISBN: 9798740795294

CONTENTS

Second Hand Computer

Jamie was a weird dude. He'd been a weird kid when David met him, and he had just gotten weirder as time went by. Still, this was his step-brother, they were family, and that meant something to folks. It meant something to David. Sure, with everybody remarrying time and time again, there was a kind of tangled web of family ties around Salisbury, but Jamie wasn't like that. They didn't spend a lot of time together now that they were grown, and honestly, they hadn't spent a ton of time together as kids either, but Jamie was always good to him. Nice even.

Nice was a hard thing to come by out here. The folks that weren't turned in on themselves had a nasty habit of lashing out hard. Life was rough, there was no denying it, but David never understood how making everyone else's life harder was meant to make him feel better about it. If that made him soft, he'd rather take the muttered insults than be the one doling them out.

It was a funny thing – Jamie should have been one of the people who came down on him the hardest. He kept it under wraps for the most part, but his family knew that he was into all that white-power neo-Nazi bully-boy stuff. He lived his whole life by that code of puffed-up machismo that was just an undercurrent for everyone else on the wrong side of the tracks. This was the kind of guy who'd spit on disabled people. Who'd happily kick a man's teeth out if he suspected he was gay. Yet there he was in the driver's seat of the truck, going out of his way by miles to give David a ride and do him a favour.

David knew that people called him faggot behind his back. They didn't do it quietly. He showed his strength in different ways – by turning the other cheek when those accusations and rumours got circulated. He knew who he was, and he didn't have to prove himself to anybody.

The taunt had upset him when he was still a teenager, and he'd come to his older brother with furious tears in his eyes after the teasing he'd suffered. Ranting about how it was disgusting. How he'd never let a man touch him like that. He wasn't weak, he wasn't pathetic, just because he didn't want to fight everyone all the time. He didn't want to be a tough guy. That didn't mean that he was less than anyone else. Jamie had just taken him at his word, stared off into space, let him get it out. There was no judgement from Jamie – the boy who judged the whole world by his black-and-white standards.

He'd always treated his step-brother well, better than their parents' seething contempt, better than the schoolboy bullying his friends offered up in place of any genuine emotional connection. It left David with a nasty little worm of guilt in his belly that he was using Jamie like this.

Okay, using was maybe too strong a word. If he told Jamie why he'd asked him to come along, then there was no doubt in his mind that the younger man would have just laughed it off and agreed, but it grated on David to even admit why he needed Jamie right now.

For all of his big talk about not needing to strut around and be a tough guy to get by in the world, he still needed a tough guy to come along with him on days like this. To stand there and look menacing, so that he could buy a second-hand computer instead of getting mugged for the cash he'd brought along. It was pathetic. He was pathetic.

He felt even worse because Jamie had made it all so easy. The minute he'd mentioned that he was in the market for a second-hand computer – planning on planting the seeds for his later request for a lift and a hand carrying it – Jamie had sprung into action, reaching out through the grapevine of pseudo-criminals that he brushed shoulders with on a daily basis to find him the best deal going.

David's budget wasn't big – as much as he held himself to a higher standard than the thugs that populated the backwaters around northern Adelaide, he was still just as poor as the rest of them – but within a couple of days, Jamie had come back to him with a little napkin with a jumble of technical information jotted down on it that it was clear the other man didn't understand a word of. Random-access memory for Jamie was flashbacks to a night when he'd been blackout drunk, not anything to do with a little hunk of electronics in a beige box.

He'd dutifully read out all of the stats even though they meant nothing to him, and David's heart sank with every new line of numbers. There was no way that he could afford a computer with specs this high on his budget. When Jamie got to the end and read out the last numbers on his napkin, the price, David was fully expecting to have an awkward conversation. Instead, he was stumped. 'How much?'

Jamie never said that it was stolen. He never even implied it. But for some reason, in the back of David's mind, the connection had been made between his brand spanking new computer with all these great components and the distinct possibility that some criminal activity had been involved in its acquisition. That maybe David was somehow complicit, or an accomplice in some way, because he'd told Jamie what he was looking for and suddenly it had materialised. As if it had just appeared out of thin air, or fallen off the back of a lorry, just because he wanted it.

So that was another little twist in David's guts as they made the long slow drive out to Snowtown. As they rolled along the road, further and further from civilisation, Jamie didn't look worried about it. But of course, Jamie wouldn't look worried about it. This was his world, all these shady people that he ended up allied with just because his politics were a little bit outside the norm. If Jamie did look worried about something, it was probably because they were already going to end up dead and chopped up in bits. The teen's face gave nothing away. He caught David staring at him and smiled at his brother. 'What? Have I got something on my face?'

For a moment, all of his little niggling worries threatened to climb right up David's throat and jump out. Jamie would take them all in his stride, laugh about the silly ones, and console him about the rest. He wouldn't lie to him, though, and if the computer was stolen, he'd trust in his stepbrother to keep his mouth shut and to keep them both out of trouble. David didn't want to know. Knowing would make this whole thing worse. If he could just pretend that everything was normal, he knew what script to follow. If it turned out to be some sort of criminal computer conspiracy, he'd be so far out of his depth he might just run off home. So, all he did was slap on a fake smile and say, 'Thanks for all this. I really appreciate it.'

Jamie leaned over and gave him a playful punch on the shoulder. 'What are family for?'

David scolded himself and deliberately turned to stare out the window. What did he have to worry about when Jamie was there with him?

The salt plains gave way to town abruptly. One main street seemed to be almost all that there was of an actual town around there. It wasn't what David had been expecting from this trip. He thought they were going to end up somewhere on the edge of nowhere outside some caravan full of dubious goods. Instead, when Jamie clapped him on the shoulder and very deliberately double-checked the address on the napkin, they seemed to be heading into an old bank.

Immediately, all of David's worries disappeared. Nothing shady and illegal ever happened in a bank! The computer that he was there to buy was probably something that the bank's corporate office sent out just before branch closure that had ended up in legal limbo. These things happened all the time. It was just the sort of legal grey area where you could get a computer this cheap.

He caught up to Jamie in a moment and walked into the dusty old building shoulder to shoulder with his stepbrother, fighting down the goofy grin that was threatening to manifest itself. All that worrying over nothing. It wouldn't do to go into this meeting with a grin like that, though. Not if he wanted them to take him seriously.

Jamie led him into the building, deeper and deeper through the empty foyers and offices until they came to a quiet wood-panelled room with a man inside. He was one of Jamie's friends. Or at least a friend of Jamie's new stepdad. That was a little bit odd, but David could come up with a dozen reasons why one of Jamie's buddies might be here if things weren't entirely legal. 'Uh. Hi. We're here about the computer?'

The man gave him a nod, which Jamie took as assent, then David turned his attention to the computer where it had been set up on the desk. The only seat was on the wrong side of the desk, but that didn't bother David one bit, not when this thing was everything that he'd been promised and more. It even had a microphone set up to do voice recordings. All he had to do was hit the button and he could record himself right now! He reached for the switch to try it out, opened his mouth and no sound came out.

Jamie's friend, the older guy with a goatee, had a hold of David by the throat. 'Not another word, faggot.'

David tried to mouth out a denial. He scrabbled involuntarily at the hands around his throat, then he saw Jamie was already reaching for them. Jamie was going to save him.

Jamie took a hold of David's wrists and pulled his arms down so that he couldn't interfere as the other man choked the life out of him. Still struggling despite his mounting horror, David tried to throw himself free of the killer grasp only for Jamie's face to loom forward suddenly out of the darkness that was encroaching, his forehead slamming down into David's soft face. Why? That was all that he could think as he slipped into unconsciousness. Why would his own step-brother do this to him?

When he finally woke up, coughing and wheezing through his bruised throat, he was tied to the chair. The microphone had been turned around to face him. Jamie, the other guy, Jamie's stepdad, and another man that David didn't know were all gathered around. Grins on their faces. Cigarette tips flaring in the dim light. He shouldn't have made a noise. The moment that they realised he was awake, Jamie stepped forward with something in his hands. David flinched, just waiting for the pain to come, but it didn't. Something was dropped onto his lap.

His hands were cuffed behind his back, but his legs were still free. He tipped the clipboard up with his knees to read what was on it. A script was written out for him. At least he wouldn't have to worry about what to say.

It was split into different sections. A declaration that he was moving away. A full confession to molesting little boys. Being gay. Being an insufferable stain on the white race. It was all there, clear as day. Scratched out in black and white as though it were the truth, even though David hadn't done a single one of the things it claimed that he did. Jamie leaned in closer until the tip of his cigarette was flaring bright an inch from David's eye.

He reached past the bound man and pressed the record button.

Senseless

On the fourth of September, 1966, in Inala, Queensland, a baby boy was born. John Justin was the first and only child of the Bunting family. Tiny, pink and perfect. His parents genuinely believed in that latter part. The perfection of their son was beyond question in their minds. The only real issue that they had was that no matter what food they prepared, they could not get him to show the slightest bit of excitement. As a baby, they struggled to get him to breastfeed, and after weaning, the boy had to be manually fed most of his meals or he'd simply lose interest. He did not gain weight like the rest of his peers, his bones still showing under his skin, while the other children in his playgroup showed a thick layer of puppy fat. It got to the point that his concerned mother finally overruled his father's insistence that there was nothing wrong with the boy and took him to a doctor for examination.

They poked and prodded at the tiny boy for hours on end, running all manner of tests until it seemed that there could be no blood left in his body and no crevice unexplored. He was almost sent along to a specialist for further checks before an older doctor snapped his fingers and brought out the old smelling salts that he'd hung onto since the fifties. They were as pungent as ever, and everyone in the doctor's office flinched away from them. Everyone except for John. He couldn't smell them. He couldn't smell anything.

Reassured that the only problem with her son was his lack of a single, mostly useless sense, his mother took him home and set about altering the menu to appeal to somebody with his limited ability to taste. Soon after, he began to pack on the pounds and develop healthily.

There was a strict order to life in the Bunting home, and while some children may have rankled at every moment of their life being scheduled, it seemed to suit John nicely. He always knew where he stood, always knew what would come next, everything in his life made sense.

The reins were loosened more and more as he grew older, and by the time that he was attending school in Inala, he was granted the freedom to manage his own time for the most part. His mother insisted that he be home for dinner at her specified time, but beyond that, he could come and go as he pleased. He was never late. In fact, he was often home exactly one minute before his mother would have demanded it of him. Routine seemed to give him comfort.

While he was a quiet child who seemed to enjoy his own peaceful company the best, John did not struggle to make friends. If anything, the very limited demands that he made on others made him more popular than needier children. He had an extensive circle of friends by the time that he was eight years old, one that encompassed most of his grade along with cousins and their friends.

This being the case, he was never short on invitations to come around and play during the long holidays from school that Australia boasted. It was during one of these playdates that he would have what he would spend the rest of his life calling 'the accident'.

The summer heat was high in 1974, and air conditioning was limited to standing fans in most homes, nowhere near up to the task of damping down the dry heat. Playing out in the streets or the parks of Inala was out of the question if the kids wanted to avoid heatstroke. Even slathered in suntan lotion, John could feel himself crisping as he made his way across town to the home of a buddy. A buddy with a nice cool basement where they could play as loudly as they wanted without anyone complaining because his parents were out at work.

All was going well in the morning. The boys played to their little hearts' content, bothering nobody but the ants that were trying to encroach on the basement. Around noon, the teenaged brother of John's friend stuck his head around the door to see what all the noise was about. It put a damper on their play for a couple of minutes as John's friend looked nervously up at the door every time that they made a noise, but John didn't think much more of it. He didn't really understand the relationships between siblings, so he tended to accept whatever happened as normal without question.

When the older brother came back, he was holding some rope. 'You babies want to play a big boy game?'

Immediately, John's friend fell quiet, looking away. It seemed to fall to John to politely reply, 'No, thank you.'

Apparently, that was the wrong answer. The teenager crossed the basement in a few strides and clubbed the eight-year-old down with one punch. He had never been hit before. He'd been in little scraps, like all boys his age, but a real punch was outside of his realm of knowledge. Even after he'd hit the ground, he wasn't sure what was going on. Just that there was a pain in his cheek, a ringing in his ear, darkness creeping in at the periphery of his vision. 'What?'

There was no confusion about the stamp that followed. It had been meant to mash his testicles, but reflexively he'd closed his legs around the descending foot and caught the brunt of it on his thighs. Ripping the skin beneath his trousers. Enraging the teenager.

John's friend tried to run, and he made it up a few of the stairs before his brother caught him by the ankle and he fell, face first, into the concrete steps. He was out cold before the teenager could drag him back down into the room and toss him in the corner between the bean bags and the fold-out sofa.

Trying to get back to his feet just made John dizzy, but he still had to try. He had to go tell. If he went and told, then the bad boy would get in trouble and he wouldn't do it again. The idea that this teenager was already well-practised in the violence that he was committing didn't even cross the boy's mind.

The teenager caught him by the hair and dragged him back into the room, yelping and wailing all the way. 'Nobody can hear you, baby.'

An open-handed slap rocked John's whole world. Things began to spin. What had been things became shapes in the world around him, hazy and meaningless, as he felt his body being tossed around, the burn of the ropes over his skin, the cool basement air on his exposed skin.

He'd been tossed on the folded-out bed, and the teenager was laughing at him. Pointing at him and laughing as he squirmed over to hide his tiny genitals from sight, shame being the only thing that seemed to be cutting through the pain and confusion. He tried to cover himself with his hands, but they were tied behind his back. He tried to draw up his legs, but they were bound, too. He managed to flop over onto his front so that the other boy couldn't see him anymore. Tears of shame pricked at his eyes as he pressed his face down into the mattress. He couldn't smell the tea-stained fold-out. Even if he had, he wouldn't have recognised the significance of the smells. He was just an innocent child.

The springs of the bed screeched and groaned as the teenager climbed onto the bed over him. Slaps rained down on his exposed backside, like the one time he'd talked back to Daddy. They stung, but compared to the beating he'd already taken, the pain barely even seemed to register. He felt the boy spitting on him, too, but after the other degradations, it was just another insult in the litany. Through it all, the teenager was ranting and rambling. Calling him every name under the sun. Saying anything and everything to make the boy upset. John had gone away inside his own head. He couldn't physically escape, but he could disappear inside, where nobody would ever be able to find him.

That was when his attacker pressed inside. First with his spit-slick fingers, then a moment later with something bigger, thicker. It burned. Oh, God, it burned. In an instant, John was back in his body. Screeching in agony as this stranger pressed inside his body.

John knew nothing of sex, and even less about homosexuality. It was not a topic of polite conversation in the Bunting household. He had no idea why the other boy was doing what he was doing or why. All that he knew was that it hurt so badly, he'd rather die than endure another minute of it. He didn't have to wait long. After just a few seconds of grunting and thrusting, the pain was over, replaced with a feeling of horrible wetness – some of it blood from where John had been torn, but the rest was something he didn't know.

There was so much that he didn't know. A whole world of horrors that were just starting to open up to him. The teenager was gone. Somewhere in the last minute or two, he'd left the room and left John tied up and leaking on the bed, screaming in pain, screaming for help, all of it useless. Senseless.

It didn't take long for the teenager to come back downstairs and smack him for screaming. He had a cold drink in his hand, and he settled himself down on one of the beanbags to wait.

Once again, they didn't have to wait long. Three more boys, all about the same age as John's friend's brother, came stamping down the stairs. Laughing and jeering and ready to take part in the day's festivities.

They took turns on John. One after the other. Interspersing their rape with other molestations. Forcing their...things into his mouth. Pinching at his body. Touching him down there where nobody was meant to see. Slapping him. Hitting him. Biting him. There was no resistance left in the little boy after his friend's brother was done with him, but still, they preceded every new degradation with a beating to soften him up. It went on for hours. A blur of pain, disgust, and other more shameful, uncontrollable sensations that would remain burned into John's soul for the rest of his life. They took their turns, then another turn if they were in the mood, then finally when they were all done, it was as though the whole world had gone quiet.

John was numb as they untied him. Numb as he pulled his trousers and pants back up. Numb as he took each step up out of the darkness of the basement with agonising care. He stepped out into the burning heat of the early evening, and he didn't even notice it. He wondered if the feeling would ever come back, and he hoped that it wouldn't. He didn't want to feel after this.

It was more than an hour after his curfew by the time that he made it home. His mother was livid. The dinner that she had prepared for the family was spoiled and thrown out. He was sent to his room without anything to eat, grounded from going out for a week.

In normal circumstances, it is quite possible that he would have baulked at such cruelty, but John had no intention of playing anyway. The thing that really pushed his mother over the edge into such draconian punishment was not that he was late, that he'd missed his dinner, that she had spent that whole hour fretting and worrying about him, it was that he would not say where he had been or what he had been doing. She had been home worried sick. Any terrible thing might have been happening to him, and he wouldn't even tell her where he had been or who he had been with? She was enraged.

Alone in the dark of his room, John tried to piece together what had happened to him. Fragments of it made sense to his eight-year-old mind, but most of it was beyond him. How could he tell his mother what had happened when he didn't know himself? How could he look her in the eye and tell her that he had been made to debase himself for the pleasure of some boys? Would anyone even believe that he had been forced? There were bruises now, bleeding too, but that would fade, and soon all that would be left was his word against that of four older boys. Would anyone believe him? And did he want to live with the shame of the whole world knowing what they had done to him? Could he stand there in front of his father and tell people how they'd put their...things inside him? How they'd whispered in his ear what a good girl he'd be?

In the days that followed, there was a marked change in little John. At first, his mother thought that he was sulking about his punishment, but even when the week ended and he was allowed out to play with his friends again, he didn't seem inclined to roam far from home. He'd never been a fearful child, and even now, he didn't seem scared of the prospect of roaming the neighbourhood so much as it had just lost its appeal. Like the part of his brain that felt excitement and joy had been switched off.

Where before there had been a spark of delight in every conversation, now John seemed to say what was expected of him by rote. Where once he would be bouncing with excitement to go and visit a friend for the day, now he seemed happier to be left to his own devices, scorching lines into the pavement with a magnifying glass. They couldn't force him to have fun, but his parents did everything in their power to get him back into his active social life, taking him to every birthday party thrown over the rest of the summer and running him down to the beach on their days off.

Everywhere that John went, the spectre of his 'accident' followed him. The four boys who had taken their turns on him seemed to be everywhere that he looked. It wasn't that small a town, but every time he went outside, he seemed to see them. Jeering at him. Smirking. One even miming some of the grotesque acts that they'd committed against him.

It didn't get better when he went back to school in autumn. The teenagers may not have been there, but they seemed to have plenty of suck-ups and lackeys who were still young enough to be in primary school, and they delighted in pointing and laughing at John, even if they'd never been told the full story of the exact indignities that those they hero-worshipped had inflicted on the boy.

Fear and rage seemed to swap back and forth. He hated them almost as much as he hated himself for letting it happen to him, but he didn't dare to lash out at them. Not when any one of them might know the whole story and let it slip.

He was cornered by his friend's brother almost a year after the 'accident'. Pinned up against a wall by the older boy's imposing frame. Shaking despite all his attempts to keep cool as memories of the last time that they had been so close replayed in his mind. 'You haven't told anybody about our little playtime, have you, baby?'

John managed to shake his head.

'That's good. Wouldn't want everyone to find out you moaned like a whore when I did it to you, would you? Wouldn't want me and my mates to come in through your bedroom window at night and do it to you all over again? I hear even a whisper about our little party in the basement, and we'll be having parties every single week. You hear me?'

It took everything that John had to drag his stare up and meet the older boy's eyes. He strained against his fear until he was looking eye to eye with his rapist.

The older boy slapped him. 'Do you hear me?'

'I hear you.' There was a growl in John's voice that even he didn't recognise. It was enough to make the older boy look back at him twice. There was no fear in little John's eyes when he stared up at the boy who'd raped him. Nothing but hate. He staggered away from the kid, then stepped back in with a fist clenched. The boy didn't even flinch. Something was not right in that boy's head.

In the months that followed, one after another, John's other rapists came forward with their own nasty little threats. He didn't brush them off, but neither did he seem all that concerned for his safety. There was nothing that they could do to him that they hadn't already done. There was nothing that they could make him feel that was worse than what he had already experienced. Whatever fear he had felt was burned away by his fury.

He no longer sat by the side of the street burning lines with the magnifying glass. Instead, he went directly to the ants' nests. He gathered them up in little jars. Carried them back to his shed and doused them in the fluids that he had secreted around there, from his junior chemistry set, from around the house. He dissolved them. Making everything melt away. When that did nothing to soothe his fury, he started throwing rocks at the neighbourhood cats until they were all afraid of him, before moving further afield to find animals that were not scared enough of him, animals that he could creep up to and capture.

As he closed his hands around them, felt their bones shift and creak and break, he imagined what it would be like to do this to the four boys who'd raped him. As he felt the little furry bodies cool, he felt a wash of guilt and shame. They had done this to him. They had made him like this.

At school, his performance began to suffer immediately, and by the age of twelve, he was near failing in every class except for chemistry, where his obsession seemed to lie. He was fascinated with the different ways that seemingly innocuous things could come together to make something dangerous or lethal.

He got into fights more and more often, practically bubbling over with aggression towards not only the other students but even his teachers. If anything, he seemed to have even more contempt towards the members of staff who were trying to make him obedient than to the people that he beat bloody for any perceived slight. In a dark basement years ago, he had learned that compliance earned him no special favours. It just made it easier for the people with power to stomp on your face while you thanked them. He was never going to be compliant again.

The carefully ordered home life that he had enjoyed up until this point crumbled when he refused to obey his mother and father in all things. He still enjoyed the structure and the order of things, but he only enjoyed them when they were on his terms. If he wanted his daily routine to be different, he made it different. If his parents tried to punish him, he took the spanking without a flinch or a word. He'd endured worse. No matter what anyone in his life ever tried to deal out to him, he had endured worse.

Conflict at home escalated when he began skipping school, and even more when he started staying out late at night. His parents feared that he might have been getting involved in underage drinking or maybe even drugs. Their once-open son had completely closed himself off from them and would tell them nothing about his life. It was like a stranger was living with them. A boy whom they did not know, who had one day killed their son and taken his place. They couldn't even talk to him about these concerns because all that it would earn them was the same contemptuous stare that he gave to teachers, the police, or anyone else who tried to tell him what to do.

John had not turned to drugs or alcohol for solace. He viewed addiction as a despicable weakness and had no desire to become an animal. Instead, he was spending his time outside the home on much more dangerous hobbies.

First Out the Gate

By his thirteenth birthday, despite all of his best efforts to stave off any sense of vulnerability, John was at the heart of a perfect storm of factors that would make him liable to be sexually abused again. He was socially isolated, directionless, desperate for someone, anyone, to give his life direction and purpose again. All it would have taken was a little bit of kindness from any stranger and he might have fallen under their spell.

Instead, he found Benny.

Usually, when an abused teenager befriends a man in his thirties, the expectation is that something sinister is going on. In this case, that was entirely correct, but the sinister happenings were not what might have been expected. The two of them met by chance during John's rambling journeys about town, and soon a conversation was struck up on the most horrible of subjects. Benny gave John a warning not to go wandering around the park where they'd met after dark because it was a notorious hook-up spot for the local gay community, and according to Benny, they would rape a pretty young thing like John as soon as look at him.

The older man had expected to scare the boy off one way or another, either letting a young gay lad looking for some business know that there was someone hostile about, or genuinely warning off some average kid that didn't know any better. He certainly didn't expect to hear the stocky kid turn around and say, 'Let them try, I'll fucking kill them.'

It was the start of a beautiful friendship or at least a hasty indoctrination. Benny was a strong believer in the supremacy of the straight white man, and he had the covert neo-Nazi tattoos to prove it. He viewed everyone else as inherently inferior and considered gay people to be among the worst offenders. Disabled people, drug users, Aboriginals, and Asians he could identify on sight, but the gays were insidious. They could look just like a 'normal' person right up until the moment that they made their true intentions clear. He'd made them the focus of his crusade against this enemy within. A war effort that had just found its latest recruit.

For several months, the man and the boy would just meet up at random spots around town, sharing cigarettes and talking about their loathing for the homosexual population – a group that the older man made no efforts to distinguish from child molesters in the mind of young John.

It did not take long before their talk turned to action. Late in the evening, well past his curfew, John would hang around near to the local gay hotspots, attempting to be propositioned. Most nights, he was. He'd then lure the wannabe Casanova down an alleyway with the implication that it would be the location of their less-than-romantic rendezvous. Deep in the shadows, far from witnesses, Benny would make it a threesome, leaping out from cover to assault the predatory men who had thought that their luck was in. The men were beaten, insulted, spat on, and robbed, yet not one of them went to the police. There was no legal risk to Benny and John at all. Not one of the men that they had transformed from predator to prey would dare to report what had lured them down into the alleyway. So, early in his life, John learned the all-important lesson that there were victims that society as a whole would secretly be glad to be rid of.

While he was still small and fairly unintimidating, John did begin to build muscle during the two years that followed, attending school intermittently for regular classes with the exceptions of chemistry and physical education, where he suddenly went from a reluctant participant to a powerhouse player, working out in the school gymnasium through breaks and lunchtime, surrounded constantly by the aroma of sweat, but completely unaware of it.

He seemed to be preparing himself for the future career of manual labour that the world was expecting of him, and his teachers, who had long since given up trying to draw the bright young boy back out of the morass of rage and contempt that John had become, viewed it as a net positive. If only they had known that the reason he was improving himself was to make him a more effective mugger.

As he grew older and more noticeably bulky, his appeal to the predators lessened. He had to start relying increasingly on his charisma and charm to get his way. Something that he proved startlingly adept at. Benny was never able to mask his disgust at 'the poofs' for long enough to carry on a conversation with them, but John was a natural-born liar. Like all of his personality and morals could be turned off with the flick of a switch when it suited his purposes.

The flow of blood and money slowed, but John's talent ensured that it didn't dry up entirely. He did his duty and he did it well, but in the back of his mind, all of the sexual attention that he was receiving from men was adding fuel to a nasty little ember of doubt that he harboured about his own sexual orientation.

The only sexual contact that he had received in his life had been from men, and the sensations of it still haunted him. Not the awful pain that he had experienced, but the awful moments when it did not hurt. The moments when it had almost felt pleasurable. While he was a late bloomer, puberty was coming on hard for John now, and the rush of hormones had prompted all of the usual self-exploration that went along with it. Sensations that until now he had only associated with his rape.

By the age of fifteen, he needed to know for certain where his true interests lay. If it was in men, then he would rather kill himself than grow up to be a molesting monster like he and Benny hunted.

While he hadn't been a major player in the social scene at his school for many years, he still had many close friends there. A smaller circle than he'd had when he was younger, certainly, but he wasn't an outcast by any means. The only reason that he had been isolated was that he had chosen to isolate himself. Between his bad-boy reputation, athletic prowess, the body that he was working hard to develop, and the air of mystery around him, there was no shortage of female attention being directed his way. All that he needed to do if he wanted to have sex was respond to their advances. Something that until this point, he'd had no real interest in doing.

He began attending parties with his friends and cousins, drinking, smoking, and generally behaving like a regular teenager for the first time in his life. It wasn't long before he was making romantic connections. Within a month, he found the opportunity to have sex with a girl for the first time, and he seized that opportunity with both hands.

While it may not have been an event for the history books, given both participants' lack of practical experience, John was still successful in his pairing, lying back in bed with a lit cigarette and a sense of peace and calm that he hadn't experienced since he was eight years old. The girl hadn't meant much of anything to him, and while he didn't exactly kick her out of bed, all of the seemingly genuine overtures of real romance that he'd been making towards her over the past few weeks vanished in an instant as soon as he got what he wanted. After that, she wanted nothing to do with him. Sadly, biology had other plans.

It was almost four months later when their paths crossed again. John was now sixteen and leaving school, getting ready to take his first steps into the larger world where he was free to live as he pleased, as an adult. She had spent almost a month tracking him down through the network of their shared friends. The baby bump was already pronounced.

There was no hesitation on John's part. He immediately offered to marry the girl who was pregnant with his child, and he was immediately shot down. She did not want him in her life, or the life of her child. All that she wanted was financial support. She'd assumed that John's family had money from the fact that he always had cash to spend—his cut of the many muggings he'd conducted over the years—and she expected to milk his family for all that they were worth. When she discovered that what they were worth wasn't much, John promised her that she was not going to struggle. He wasn't happy with her decision to raise the child alone, but neither was he going to leave his little baby destitute. He made arrangements to pay her child support at the rate she demanded and then immediately went out and got the first job that he could find that would pay him enough to get out from under his parents' roof and pay for his kid.

The local crematorium seemed to be constantly short of staff as none of the locals wanted to work there. John wasn't so squeamish. If anything, he was too comfortable with the dead bodies, snapping out gold fillings for resale whenever he had the opportunity to prepare a corpse on his own. Despite suspicions that he was interfering improperly in the remains that he prepared, there was never enough evidence to cost John his job. The fact that even at sixteen he had the physical strength to move coffins and corpses around on his own meant that, even if there had been some proof that he was up to no good, it would likely have been overlooked. The rest of the staff trended elderly, and having an able-bodied young man about the place made a world of difference.

Throughout all of this upheaval in his life – becoming a father, moving into an apartment with some friends, and finding a job – his crusade with Benny had continued. Yet, as the days went by, he heard from his old skinhead friend less and less frequently. Before long, he had to resort to showing up to the older man's house to drag him out to do some of their good work together.

Benny never explained why he had lost his fire, and John didn't want to ask. The older man never wanted to show weakness, not even in what it turned out was going to be the last year of his life. Eventually, the truth came out when Benny's usual raspy monologues about the evils of other races slowed to an intermittent comment here and there. He was forced to admit to the boy that he had throat cancer, and that it wasn't going to be getting any better.

As Benny's condition deteriorated, John made sure to be at his side, even though he loathed hospitals with an almost ideological passion. Even at the very end of his life, as he lay in the hospital bed withering away, John was still there. The only person who was there for him, slipping him a lit cigarette when the nurses weren't about and even holding it to the man's lips when he lost the strength to do it himself. One day, Benny fell asleep and just didn't wake up. John went on visiting for a couple of days, expecting the old man to be bright-eyed and bitter as always to have missed his protégé's visits, but it never happened. Benny never did wake up, and John's crusade against the perverts and monsters of the world seemed like it was at an end before it had really begun.

He collected the specialist literature from Benny's apartment before the landlord could sweep through and trash it all. Some magazines, but mostly newsletters, typed and photocopied for distribution throughout Australia. The movement, boiled down to its barest bones. He took it home and left the less unsavoury papers scattered around where his flatmates and friends would be able to find them and start their own journey into a more enlightened state.

Without the bright bloody evenings on the town to look forward to, John started spending more and more time with his friends, drinking and laughing at their jokes. Trying to be normal, even though he knew that there were monsters out there hurting children. It got to the point that all he had to say was the word paedophile and the whole flat would start groaning and throwing things at him. They said it was the only thing that he'd talk about. An obsession.

Life might have gone on like that forevermore for John and his mates, drinking away their evenings and working hard jobs through the day, but a clash of disruptive events in their lives would soon end this little oasis of normality.

John's baby, now two years old, got to see him every once in a while. Not because the court had mandated it, but because the mother could often milk him for a little extra cash if she softened him up with some playtime first. He knew she was doing it, of course, but he didn't begrudge his little boy anything. Even if he couldn't be a part of his life, that was his son.

He was almost surprised when his ex-lover sent the kid off to play and held John back to speak to him ahead of that time together. She must have known that her routine worked or she wouldn't have kept it up for two years, so why was she messing up a good thing now?

As it turned out, this wasn't their normal meeting. This was a chance for John to say goodbye. She wasn't going to need his child support money any more, but he wasn't going to be seeing them anymore, either. The two of them were moving to England, on the opposite side of the world. He would never see either one of them again.

He was stunned and furious with her in turns. There was no way that he could have predicted this. While he shared a few choice words with the mother of his child, the equilibrium of his life, already shaken after the death of Benny, was knocked completely off-kilter. It threw his whole life into stark relief. Without the baby to support, he had no real need for the job at the crematorium. He had nothing at all tying him to Inala anymore.

At the very same time, all of John's friends were making their own transitions. Some were leaving school. Some were finding that the hard work expected of manual labourers did not appeal to them and were failing their way towards unemployment. Others were seeing longstanding romantic entanglements falling apart in the time of flux. His buddy Kevin Reid was the first one to suggest just getting out of town, but John was the one to champion it. Riling them all up with stories of the opportunities that they could find beyond the borders of their crappy little hometown. A plan began to form. The group would sell off their respective belongings, pool their resources, buy a car, and make the drive across to the West Coast, where they'd have prospects beyond the drudgery that their fathers endured.

Out of a sense of duty, John made one last visit to his parents to say goodbye, but by this point, the abyss between them had widened to the point that the only conversation they could muster was a listing of the facts. He was leaving. He wasn't coming back. He'd call once he was settled to let them know where he was in case any mail came. That was it. The sum of their relationship.

Loading up one box each, the kids climbed into the second-hand banger that they'd managed to secure for the scarce funds they'd been able to raise. The more sensible among them were overruled when it was suggested that they hold on, raise more money, remove the element of risk. John treated any measure of sanity as cowardice. Raining contempt down on the nay-sayers. This was their chance to get out.

All of his life, for as long as he could remember, he'd been feeling the walls closing in around him. Every time somebody looked at him, he had to wonder if they knew. If they knew what had been done to him. If the story had been shared around by his rapists to raucous laughter in the social circles of perverts. So long had passed that John wouldn't have even recognized the boys, now grown men, if he'd met them. Trauma had stripped him of so many of his memories of that day, and the healing properties of time had whittled away at the rest. Every time he passed a man in the street, he had no way of knowing if he was one of the ones who'd done it. Even back in his gay-bashing days with Benny, he'd eyed every victim with curiosity. Was this one of them? Would this be his chance to finally get some measure of justice? He'd never know. He'd never know if he'd gotten them. He'd never know if they were standing right beside him in the pub. As long as he stayed put, there was never going to be any peace.

The road trip did not go smoothly. None of the kids were experienced drivers, none of them knew the terrain, the road, they barely even knew the direction that they were heading half of the time. With precious little money scraped together, they hadn't wanted to waste any of it on a road map, trusting instead to the road signs to guide them on their way.

When they weren't going in circles, they weren't making much progress, and when they were going in circles, it didn't take long for them to realise it and turn on each other. If it weren't for the fact that abandoning someone on the side of the road was almost certainly a death sentence in the Australian outback, it was quite likely that the group of teens would have parted ways many times over.

Time was not an issue. They had nowhere to be, and all of their lives to get there, but the ever-mounting costs of their trip were like a millstone around their necks. Every dead end or wrong turn ate into their petrol. Every night that they spent camped out on the roadside was free, but the ones in towns—the softer ones among them wanted motel rooms. Even sharing head to toe, crammed into a single double bed, that cost more money than they had to waste.

They drifted further and further off course, heading south instead of west, towards the safer paved roads that didn't have them bouncing up from every pothole to bang their heads on the hot metal of the roof. Safety and smooth roads would not take them west.

The money dwindled. The fuel meter ticked over until it was in the red. They had to push the car into a town more than once, only to top up the tank just enough to leapfrog along to the next little slice of nowhere. Over and over, day after day, night after night, until finally, they found themselves in Adelaide.

It was everything that they'd dreamed of when they were making their grand plans of escape. A booming town with fresh faces everywhere they looked and, more importantly, work. Jobs were being handed out like gumdrops, just for the asking. Every one of them had a job by the end of their first day in Adelaide. Any dreams of lounging around and living off the nest egg they'd gathered had burned away in the outback. Some of them found bar work, one of the girls a gig in a shop, there was even well-paid labouring work on the building sites for those that wanted it. John didn't want it.

Down all the streets paved with gold, he trudged along completely blind, eyes searching for what the others couldn't see. The secret signs. The limp wrists. The smiles and glances that lasted just a little too long to be properly manly. They were here. He knew they were here, because they were everywhere, hiding in plain sight just like old Benny always used to say.

The city was different, but people were the same everywhere, and in less than half an hour, he had every one of them marked. He knew their hangouts, he knew their bars, he knew what to look for. It made his knuckles itch. They weren't even hiding it here. They went out dressed like...what they were. Holding hands. Making eyes at each other. Giggling. John's stomach turned over at the sight of it. They weren't afraid of being caught here. They walked past a policeman on the beat without even glancing up from their whispered conversations.

The old system would not work in Adelaide. It was too open, too bright, too liberal. If he mugged some man coming out of a gay bar, the police would probably be at his door the next day. If he picked somebody at random coming out of the gay bar, they might even be police. He'd always known that authority couldn't be trusted, but here, he could see clearly that the predators and paedophiles were now hand in hand with the law. Nobody was going to do anything to stop them. They weren't even afraid to be exposed as the monsters they were. They were proud of it. They were out in the streets kissing.

The day was dragging on, and John was still unemployed. He might have been shocked and appalled by what he had seen, but practicality still ruled him. Without a job, he wouldn't be able to sign onto a lease. All of his friends were partnering up and finding apartment spaces. If he didn't hurry up, he was going to end up spending the night sleeping in the car, and likely a lot longer than just the one night if none of them could sublet. He had to get work immediately.

Afterwards, he couldn't say for sure what had led him to the abattoir. Whether it was the blood, the screams, or the regular-looking people that he saw the further he went into the meatpacking district. Something about it felt more like home to him than anywhere else in the shining town.

Abattoirs were hiring all over town. Most of the livestock in South Australia passed through the town on its way to the restaurants and shops of the world, but the one that John walked through the door of was the South Australia Meat Corporation.

There were no stringent requirements for workers. As long as you could hold a knife, the odds were they could find a job for you somewhere. Yet in the hour's trial that they gave to John that night, testing him out at different stations, they were impressed by his talent for the work. With a knife in his hand, he moved with a confidence and skill that reminded his new supervisor of a professional chef. So quick that the eye could barely follow it.

The real test came at the start of the production line, of course. There were plenty of men who couldn't stomach the brutal reality of what they did in this place, taking living, breathing animals and turning them into cuts of meat. John was not one of those men. He viewed the slaughter of animals with the same dispassion with which others might have treated filing paperwork. He cut throats without flinching. Used the bolt-gun on the bigger animals that they worried would kick out as if he'd been born to the job. Everyone in management thought that it was their lucky day.

With a signed contract in hand, John caught up to his other friends and managed to beg a bedroom from Kevin Reid and his girlfriend. Neither of them had secured a job that paid half as well as John was being promised. If they had to keep it down a bit when they went to bed and had to let him sleep on the couch so that they had drinking money, it was hardly a great imposition. Not after weeks with their backsides all pressed together in the back of a car. They already all stank like each other – what was a little more cohabitation after all that? The fact that they were still speaking to each other at all was miraculous, so they may as well push their luck a little further.

They actually got on surprisingly well once they'd all had a shower and a sleep on something softer than the bed of a truck. The excitement of the new lives that they were starting carried them through the first few weeks of living paycheque to paycheque and scrabbling to buy milk, and before they knew it, they had all settled comfortably into the new routine.

While friends living together rarely ended with them remaining friends, both John and the couple he was housing with were surprisingly lenient with the others. They all appreciated the newfound freedom they'd discovered away from the watchful eyes of their parents, and none of them felt inclined to curb the freedom of the others.

With the money he wasn't drinking, John began collecting weaponry, ordered by mail from the back pages of his neo-Nazi magazines, surprising nobody. He developed an interest in metalwork, started purchasing tools, and looked into courses at the local community colleges.

Meanwhile, Kevin and his girlfriend became increasingly domestic, spending their income decorating the place with non-lethal items and even buying a puppy so that they could play at being a family.

John did not like the dog and the dog did not like John. Something about him seemed to set its hackles up. Maybe it smelled the death on him, carried home from the slaughterhouse each night. Maybe it recognised the predatory glint in his eyes when he looked at it.

He spent all day every day killing animals now, but the thrill was gone for him. Cutting a throat or firing a bolt wasn't nearly the same as the elaborate torments he used to inflict on the cats and dogs in his parents' neighbourhood.

It wasn't enough. He wasn't getting his fix.

While everyone around him settled into a life of quiet mediocrity in this great new city, John did not. The same restless energy that had run him out of town was still hovering around him like a great buzzing cloud of static, sparking off to strike his friends once in a while and setting them back into action when it seemed there would be nothing in their future but the nine to five and an infinite stretch of evenings and weekends of beers by the barbecue.

It didn't matter how good John was at his job, how widely he was praised, or how adored he was by his friends and co-workers. He was incapable of being satisfied. He needed more. It wasn't enough. Nothing was ever going to be enough.

At first, it seemed like John might take a step away from his criminal past and nightmarish impulses and turn all that restless energy into genuine growth as a person. He took up metalworking at the local college, paying his way and developing a new set of skills that he thought might grant him some upward mobility. Maybe even a chance at a quiet life out in the suburbs all of his very own.

For reasons both obvious and more socially complex, abattoir workers weren't exactly considered to be prime bachelor material in Adelaide. There was a stigma against the people in the more rural areas around town, and the townies' closest point of contact with most of those rural people was the abattoirs. Veronica Tripp would not have given a slaughterhouse boy a second look if she had first met him in context, but at the college night classes, she saw nothing of the country in John. He was diligent, attentive, head of the class in many ways, with an active interest in understanding the things that other people just took for granted. It wasn't enough for him to know that the pre-packaged cans of compressed gas would get a blowtorch burning hot enough to cut steel, he needed to know the composition of the gasses, the degree to which they were compressed. Everyone else seemed to be training for a bottom-rung job in some work crew, while John seemed to be learning some secret art form that was going over everyone else's head.

There was an undeniable charisma to John, or at least an intensity that was easy enough to mistake for it. He approached everything with absolute focus, and to be on the receiving end of that laser-guided attention was flattering to many people. Like they were important by association. As important as the gas-air mix, certainly.

Veronica was drawn to him, and even his non-traditional living situation with Kevin and his girlfriend did nothing to temper that passion. She could see great things in John's future, and that was a future that she wanted to be a part of. The two of them were married after a whirlwind courtship of only a few months. The courthouse wedding and the reception sprawling across all the nearby bars were attended by hundreds of people. Some were the friends that Veronica had spent a lifetime accruing in the city of her birth, but the vast majority were just people that had crossed John's path once or twice and been caught up in his wake. That intensity had come into play again. A short talk with him could make the casual conversationalist feel like they were best friends.

Co-workers and even his bosses at the meat company came out in droves to celebrate his big day, and by the end of it, Veronica was so caught up in the excitement of the new life she could see shimmering on the horizon that she didn't even realise she'd be spending the night sleeping on a sofa.

The newlyweds made do for as long as they could, but before long, their combined income had them pushing Kevin to move out into a bigger place where they could all find a room of their own. Veronica knew just how bad some of the suburbs of Adelaide were, but in her mind, it was a temporary compromise to give them some breathing space before John made his great breakthrough – whatever that might be – and lifted them off the bread line and into the lap of luxury. He had been stockpiling tools and equipment in preparation for graduating from his metalworking class. Ready to launch into a new career just as soon as they got moving.

Unfortunately, there was a degree of reluctance to move, exacerbated by the comfortable little life that Kevin and his girlfriend had assembled for themselves. They knew that John wouldn't leave them in the lurch – he was too good a guy to do something like that. He might have been a bit uncomfortable on the sofa with his wife, but he wasn't going to move out and leave them owing a rent that was too big for them, not when it was his fault they'd picked a place that they couldn't afford without him to start with because he'd been so desperate for someplace to stay.

Day in, day out, John worked his shifts, took his night classes, drank a few beers, and repeated the cycle. It was like he'd stalled out. All of the dreams he'd been building toward became more distant. All of the boundless energy he had to give was turned back inward.

His shifts and their shifts rarely lined up. He barely saw his wife, and any hint of romance was drained away by the other couple in the room. The only constant in his life was coming home to a cold and empty house, with only the dog that hated him for company.

The feeling was mutual. That dog became a symbol of everything that was wrong in John's life. The stagnating power of the domestic situation that Kevin had committed himself to, given flesh and four legs. Every day the dog growled at him, every day he growled right back. It was almost a joke. Right up until the moment that it wasn't.

John knew exactly the right gas-to-air mix to make his new blowtorch burn the hottest. He knew just the way to handle it so that he could feel every little vibration in the gear, so he could tell without looking just how everything was working. All that he didn't know, and all that he desperately craved to know, was how flesh would part beneath the dagger of heat.

The dog was yapping away, nobody was around, he was bored, he was tired. There were no good reasons, but a million excuses, all of them to justify the simple fact that he wanted to make something hurt.

At the first touch of blue-white flame, the dog snapped at him, and that gave him all the justification that he needed to turn the blowtorch on its face, searing fur and flesh away. Dribbling juices and slobber to the carpet.

It tried to run, but shock was already setting in. He caught it by a hind leg and dragged it back into range of the torch. He burned lines down it until he could see bone beneath the blackened crisp hide. The dog died sometime in the middle of his impromptu barbecue, but he didn't notice. John's attention never wavered from the bright smoking point where fire met flesh.

Before the rest of the household came home, he buried the dog out back. There were questions, of course there were questions, and John told Kevin that there was an accident with the blowtorch. Never really making the effort to sound convincing or to shut down the hysterical cries from Kevin's girlfriend that he'd always hated the dog. That it was deliberate, that John had done it on purpose. She was upset, hysterical, nobody believed that John would do something so evil. Through it all, John gave no word in his defence. All his usual acerbic wit was missing. He bore the onslaught without flinching or lying to make things easier on himself. That more than anything else had Kevin and Veronica convinced that it was all some accident that had left the man they cared for traumatized. John, who could talk his way out of anything, sitting silent. It was hard to believe.

When that storm had passed, and Kevin's girl finally admitted that John would never hurt an animal even if he didn't get along with it, things were different. The air of camaraderie and the sense that nothing would ever change were gone. The bubble had been quite effectively burst, and they began to drift their separate ways. Kevin spoke seriously about finding a place of his own, and John was supportive. This was what he'd been wanting for months. A clean break.

John and Veronica found a place to call their own at 203 Waterloo Corner Road, in the suburb of Salisbury North, just outside of Adelaide.

It was everything that they wanted, and everything that they should have been trying to avoid in one package. The house itself was a sprawling bungalow much bigger than they needed and almost inexplicably cheap until the area was taken into account. Salisbury wasn't just on the wrong side of the tracks; it was through the looking glass. The wealthy of Adelaide might have turned their noses up at working men like John and his friends, but they wouldn't have even been able to look the underclass that dwelled in Salisbury North in the eye.

Community and hope were the foundations on which a working civilization could be built, and Salisbury North had neither one. People did not reach out a hand of friendship for fear of it being cut off. They did not help each other, because it might be taken as a sign of softness, a weakness that the predators of the neighbourhood might prey upon. Drugs, crime, disability, and illness were prevalent, but they were all just symptoms of the extreme poverty that afflicted the area. People did not have jobs, because working required having something worth working toward. There was no future for the average Salisbury North resident, no possibility of the social contract being fulfilled. If they worked, their money would either be stolen or consumed in some attempt at escape from the drudgery of the reality they were condemned to. If they didn't work, they were looked down on as subhuman by a society that had climbed the ladder to comfortable living, then kicked it out behind them.

In short, it was the kind of dog-eat-dog world that required a level of mental fortitude or outright madness to survive in. John thrived there.

Meet the Neighbours

Barry Lane returned to his house on Bingham Road years before John and Veronica arrived the next street over. He had just finished serving a prison term for sexually abusing two twelve-year-old boys, and he intended to keep a low profile as much as was humanly possible for a six-foot-tall man who regularly dressed in women's clothing.

Both Barry and his alter-ego Vanessa were a common sight on the streets and bars of Salisbury North. A common, and loathed, sight. It was a testament to just how tough Barry was that he could walk about in an area so fiercely dominated by macho culture without fear. His reputation preceded him, and in a place rife with criminals, his crimes barely even seemed to raise an eyebrow, even among the people that knew of them.

Robert Wagner was thirteen years old when he first met Barry Lane. A little older than the man's previous victims, but still a good fit. The only difference between this bout of sexual abuse and the one that saw Barry Lane jailed was that Robert wasn't just consenting, he was enthusiastic.

Over several months, Robert would run away from home, only to be discovered living with Barry again and again. Barry would never involve himself in the Wagners' 'family matters', so in an odd way, he actually became something of an ally to the young boy's parents, even as he was having sex with their child. If they reported him to the police, then the next time that Robert ran away, there was no telling where he might end up. If they left things as they stood, every time that Robert ran away from them, he could be tracked down with a phone call.

The situation in the Wagner home was abusive. It would have to be pretty unpleasant for the young Robert to consider the none-too-gentle attentions of Barry Lane as a palatable alternative. He bore a multitude of scars from his father's violence, and he shed weight like a towel being wrung out each time he was away from Barry's home and the regular filling meals that the older man cooked for him while they 'played house'.

The ultimate and most damning testament to how little Robert's parents cared about him was that eventually they just gave up. The intervals between his running away from home and their arrival on Barry's doorstep stretched out until finally they just didn't turn up at all. Relinquishing any claim on their son to the man who preyed upon him.

It was far from the average relationship, but as the years rolled on, it became less obviously twisted. Yes, Barry was still a sexually aggressive cross-dresser who liked to play at being Robert's 'wife', but once time had evened out the age difference between them, that became more or less acceptable. Or at least no worse than the vast majority of the romantic relationships in Salisbury North.

John Bunting's opinions on homosexuals were no secret, so Veronica was genuinely surprised when she saw him striding off to greet Robert in the street when they first arrived in Salisbury North. The young man was quiet, introverted, and read to her as one of the many closeted homosexuals that John had been so quick to point out to her through their time together. Yet John's bubbling enthusiasm seemed to wash right over that. He saw something in the younger man. Something all too familiar in the way that Robert's eyes darted about in search of danger.

The two became fast friends almost instantly. For Robert, it was like he was meeting an older version of himself. A version that had managed to come to peace with the suffering and cruelty of the world and emerge from it stronger rather than beaten and broken. In John, he saw hope for his future.

John was never entirely open about what he saw in Robert in return. There was some sense of kinship, certainly. Both men referred to the other as 'brother' quite frequently, despite any actual connection between them. John had a habit of befriending everyone that he met, so none of this stood out to Veronica as particularly unusual, at least not immediately.

Once they were settled into their new, spacious home, John invited Robert and his 'fiancé' around for dinner almost immediately, and Veronica had a horrible glimpse of an evening going terribly awry.

There was Robert on their doorstep with a six-pack of beer, and right behind him, smiling away with lipstick still smeared about his mouth, was Barry Lane. For a moment, they all stood there, Veronica's smile slipping, dread starting to set in on Robert's face, obliviousness still plastered all over Barry's almost as thick as his makeup. Then John ducked his head around the door, saw the two of them standing there, and said, 'You brought beer?! Cheers!'

The fact that the fiancé of the young man that he'd met and befriended only a day before seemed to be a forty-year-old man didn't even seem to register for John. His focus was almost entirely on making sure that Robert felt welcome and enjoyed their evening together.

Lane was crass, bordering on unpleasant, throughout the whole meal, but if he'd thought that he could make John uncomfortable in his own home, he was in for a surprise. No matter how lewd he made even the simplest conversation sound, John either ignored it entirely or went a step further. In a strange way, he earned the begrudging respect of Lane by not trying to ignore the elephant in the room or to downplay the relationship between the two men.

During the get-together, fragments of the men's history came out. The young age at which Robert had been brought under Barry's wing made Veronica gasp in dismay, but for John, it just seemed like an affirmation that everything was as it should be. Everything was as he suspected from the start.

Even when they settled down to watch the football on television after dinner and John walked in on Robert and Barry entwined with each other, the worst that it earned them was a nudge and a laughing suggestion that they should 'get a room'.

Despite the freak show unfolding in her living room, Veronica could not drag her eyes away from John. Of all the weird and grotesque things that were being discussed, she could see nothing stranger than the way that John could not be fazed by it. She knew that he hated gay people. She knew that he hated paedophiles most of all. His rants on the topic were practically legendary, and his cold and furious descriptions of the things that he'd like to do to those men who abused children had been enough to bring social events to a dead stop.

Yet somehow, being here in this room with Barry Lane was not provoking the temper that she knew John had. It was like he had been replaced by a stranger who looked like her husband but shared none of his values.

The two visitors departed arm in arm, and Veronica turned to John, brimming with questions. He stopped her with one cold glare. It gave her shivers. It was like the mask of humanity had entirely slipped off John and she could finally see the cold dark core of hate at his centre. 'He'll get his. Don't you worry.'

The flamboyant 'Vanessa' and his young concubine were not the only neighbours that John made the acquaintance of in December of 1991 as the Bunting family settled into their new home. It did not take him long to develop a circle of friends that enveloped most of the street and surrounding area. Like a military commander claiming territory, Bunting shored up relationships to ensure that he had eyes and ears everywhere. At the time, there was no sinister motive that could be discerned. He just seemed to be a friendly, charismatic guy who wanted to get along with everybody.

The disenfranchised rejects of society had fallen through the cracks to land in Salisbury North, and John buddied up to them all: the mentally disabled, the queer, those with politics so far out of the norm that mainstream society couldn't even tolerate hearing them speak in public. They were his people. A degenerate little gang just waiting for their ringleader to arrive.

Mark Haydon became a friend to John and a regular visitor to the Bunting household. Of all the relationships that John fostered with his neighbours, Mark seemed to be the only vaguely normal one. They had a few beers, enjoyed a barbecue together, watched sports, and they spoke about relatively sane and normal topics. Of all of them, he seemed to be the least shaped by trauma, the most normal man to live on the lowest rung of society.

Beyond Mark, a few other neighbours made regular appearances in the social events of the group. Suzanne Allen and her tenant Ray Davies would show up. Their relationship was as tangled and complex as any you could find in the neighbourhood. Ray was mentally disabled and required at least some degree of support from his 'landlady', who rented him a caravan on her property, just to survive. His rent payments were inconsistent, and in the past, Suzanne had decided to take payment in the form of sexual satisfaction, creating yet more confusion in Ray's mind about the nature of their relationship.

In his inner circle, John kept his friends close and enemies closer. Robert Wagner was his closest confidante, slowly drawn out of the questionable intimacy of his relationship with Barry by the potential for a much more potent intellectual match with John. Barry Lane was always at his side, bobbing along, almost bemused by the loathing that sometimes radiated off John. It fascinated the older man, trying to work out exactly how far he'd have to push before John finally snapped. It seemed that the other man's patience was limitless. Right up until the moment that it abruptly wasn't.

Clinton Trezise was another of the local men who fell in with John, but unlike the others, he did not seem to be so completely taken in. He would socialize freely with the circle that John had gathered around himself, but when the conversation took a turn to the vitriolic, he would often excuse himself. John felt like he had no control over the man. Robert, Mark, and Ray were caught up in the cult of personality around John, dedicated in their way to his ideals and his holy war against child molesters. Lane was not dedicated to the cause for obvious reasons, but he could tell which way the wind was blowing, and as long as John tolerated his presence and let him keep his hooks in Robert, at least partially, then the relationship could be maintained.

The accusations started small. Little jibes at Clinton that weren't immediately obvious about anything. John would call him 'happy pants' as if it meant anything at all. He would repeat the things that Clinton said when the man left, affecting a lisp and a limp wrist, to much hilarity among the rather infantile audience that he'd gathered. It went on and on, little snipes. Little comments. Never enough to start a fight, but enough to make the hair on the back of Clinton's neck stand up. Like he was standing right where a lightning bolt was about to strike. It wouldn't be until August of the following year that the thunderclap would be heard.

John's employment at the abattoir had begun to slip away from him as his attention waned. The man who had been on track to be the company's top employee just seemed to vanish overnight as he turned to satisfy his urges instead of working towards building a better future for himself and his wife.

Some of it was the company that he kept rubbing off on him. None of his social circle were gainfully employed, nor did any of them show any intention of seeking a job in the near future. They almost gleefully taught John how to work the benefits system to his advantage, but in a matter of days, John's superior intellect began to shine through, and the flow of information reversed. Soon he was teaching them better ways to get access to government money, and officially left his job at the meat factory to 'sub-contract' and get paid under the table on top of the variety of other sources of income. He had no shame or guilt about working the system to his advantage, just a Darwinian contempt for those who didn't have the intelligence to do the same.

The other, less obvious but far more profound, reasons for his abandoning his post were that his plans for the future had abruptly changed. The more time that he spent in Salisbury North, the more that he learned about how life was lived there, and the more that he became convinced that the den of despair and destitution was, in fact, an opportunity just waiting for a savvy enough operator to come along and exploit it. Killing animals in the sterility of the factory had ceased to bring him pleasure. Working long, hard hours for a paycheque that he could see the government handing out to every subhuman in his neighbourhood had lost its appeal.

While he was still too young to know for certain what he wanted for the future, he felt certain that there was a way to indulge his true passions.

Veronica was not happy about this change in her husband, but it was hard to argue with a man who could logically and methodically shut down every possible angle of attack. He wasn't working anymore, but he was bringing in the same money. They had not lost the opportunity for a better future by his abandoning his role as a corporate slave when there was no way that he would ever be able to progress up the social strata even if he did advance in the company. Despite all of this, she brought the same complaints to John's door with regularity and began to withdraw her affections, since he was no longer working towards the betterment of them all.

So it was that Clinton, John, Barry, and Robert were lingering around the house watching television in the middle of the day, as they spent most days doing.

Barry had been in top form all day, throwing his 'deviant' lifestyle in John's face at every opportunity and clinging to Robert's arm when a dangerous glance was cast his way. Barry lived for those moments when he could push his luck, drive John up the wall, dole out a little bit of punishment for the ground that he'd had to cede in Robert's life as John came to dominate the young man's thoughts.

As long as Robert and Barry were together, the mincing old child molester was beyond John's reach, and they all knew it. It was part of the reason that Robert was still with the man – he feared what might become of his fiancé without manly protection.

John could not and would not attack Barry, but his frustration had built to a peak. His usual outlets had all been cut off from him, and the rage that had become the core of his personality ever since his rape had to be unleashed or it would start to turn back inward and devour him. He would not go back to feeling like that. He would not go back to being weak and afraid.

He started taking his usual pot-shots at 'happy pants'. Clinton rolled his eyes and brushed it off, the same as usual, but this time, John didn't let him fob him off with a laugh. 'You think it's funny, do you? You think it's funny to touch little kids that can't protect themselves?'

With no idea what was being spoken about, in no small part because John's vile accusations were purely the product of his fevered imagination, Clinton was forced to respond with the only tool he had in his verbal toolbox. 'Fuck off!'

John, promptly, did just that, darting out of the room while Clinton turned to the other two men with an incredulous look on his face. 'What the–'

His question was cut off by the deafening clatter of steel on bone. John came storming back into the room from the hallway with a shovel in his hands, swinging it before he'd even come into the room and catching Clinton across the back of the head. 'Fuck off? Fuck you!'

The man fell from his spot on the sofa to land face down on the carpet, blood already oozing out from the dip where his fractured skull was pressed into his brain. His body twitched spasmodically, and John hefted the spade once more, making very deliberate eye contact with Barry as he barked again, 'Fuck you.'

Whistling, the spade came down again. John was a man of compact strength, compounded by years of hard labour. When the spade hit the back of Clinton's head, the front of his face collapsed under the force of the impact. Even his teeth were knocked out of place.

Immediately, Robert leapt to his feet screaming, but Barry knew better. He'd been in dangerous situations often enough in his life to realise that the cool head wins out. He caught ahold of his boyfriend and dragged him back onto the sofa. Murmuring softly to him to calm and silence him.

They were all equally screwed, as of that moment. It didn't matter that John was the one to murder the man in front of them, Barry was an ex-con, and not the kind that anyone was going to look on with any sort of sympathy.

Both he and John would end up in jail, guaranteed, and then Robert would be alone in the world, trying to fend for himself. He'd be easy pickings for the first hard man that came along. John met Barry's eyes. It was like looking in a mirror. That same maddening grin that Barry had plastered on his face all through the year they'd spent time together. The look that said, 'Go on. Do something. I dare you.'

John had done something.

When the initial bout of hyperventilation had passed, Barry immediately put Robert to work fetching the tools they'd need.

If the boy had time to think, he'd panic. They needed to keep moving forward. Like a shark, if they stopped, they died. Barry had his car outside. Under John's watchful eye, and without any prompting, the lovers went to work, cutting away the bloodstained stretch of carpet and rolling it up around Clinton's still-warm corpse. 'Nice one, lads. That's one less paedo on the streets. The world just got a little bit better.'

For a long moment, it seemed like Robert was going to argue. He was obviously distraught and horrified at what had happened. Rage and disgust were bubbling just under the surface. If he started to fight John, then they were all screwed again, but there was nothing that Barry could do to stop him. If nothing else, he'd throw down with the murderous maniac if it might protect his boy from harm. He'd lose the fight, almost certainly. Even the two of them together just weren't built for this kind of violence.

It only took a glance at his expressionless face to know that John would kill them both, clean up the mess, and go on with his life blissfully unbothered. This was not his first time inflicting violence on this scale. There wasn't even a hint of adrenaline tremors in his hands as he brought a cigarette up to his lips and lit it. He was cool as a cucumber. He'd just beaten a man to death with a shovel, and he looked more bored than anything else. Like he was waiting for them to get on with things so that he could go on with his day. Like the corpse on the floor was an inconvenience and they were dawdling in getting it taken care of.

Both Barry and John stood frozen in the moment, waiting to see which way Robert was going to jump, the tension so thick it seemed to slow the movement of the air through the room. Robert nodded. He accepted the absurd new reality that John was pitching to him as fact. John was the hero of this story, killing a monster to protect children from harm. He had to be. Nobody would kill another human being just because they were bored. It was too deranged a possibility to even be entertained.

There had to be a reason John had done what he did. There had to be. Otherwise, nothing made sense.

The trio and their unfortunate cargo took the A1 north out of town, the three of them crammed together in the front of the pickup. Usually, Barry would have used an opportunity like this to draw Robert onto his lap, to make lascivious comments and push at the limits of John's patience. Not today. Whatever curiosity he had about the man's patience had been effectively ended the moment he saw what lay beyond that limit.

John was the one to drive, as he always did. Before, his desire to be in control of things, in the driver's seat all the time, had seemed like an odd little idiosyncrasy. Now it spoke to what the other men had both seen hiding behind that control. They weren't just happy for John to be in control, they were desperate for John to stay in control.

The road rolled by and the day dragged on, but still, John didn't slow or stop. He went on and on and on until the sun dipped down below the horizon, and then finally, after what felt like days, he swerved off into the outback. Just barely in sight of the dim glow of the Lower Light township.

John might have felt compelled to lord it over the other two back in the house, but here he re-asserted himself as one of the lads, ready to get his hands dirty in a more literal way. It was a good thing, too, as Barry was not the best when it came to manual labour. A shallow grave was dug and the remains of 'happy pants' were tossed into it with all the ceremony most men reserve for tossing out a sack of rubbish. No words were spoken over him. No sorrow was expressed. John wouldn't have tolerated any sort of sentiment.

The paedophile was the enemy, subhuman and monstrous. He'd made that clear enough in his many pointed rants through the time that they'd known him. Rants that now began to feel like accusations to Barry. He had never been sure if John knew about his past convictions, or if the pointed remarks about paedophiles deserving to be castrated were only in reference to his relationship with Robert.

Regardless, his entire attitude changed from that day forward. He no longer tried to prickle John. He essentially rolled over and showed his stomach whenever the two of them disagreed on anything. It wouldn't take long for this abrupt lack of backbone to take its toll on his relationship with Robert. John spent more and more of his apparently boundless free time with the younger man, and now that Barry was unwilling to push back against him, it soon brought the May–December romance to an end.

Affair Trade

While John found some affirmation of his life choices in the murder of Clinton Trezise, Veronica did not. She was unaware of his crime. All that she knew was that she returned home to find her husband and her carpet missing. By the time that he came rolling in at three in the morning, reeking of beer, she didn't even have to demand any excuses. Not that John ever made excuses anyway. Not when he could just give her a smug smirk and ignore all the things that were upsetting her.

She couldn't leave him. Not because of the social pressures that would have stopped a couple just a decade before from separating, but because of that same charismatic intensity that had won her over in the first place. No matter that he might behave like just another one of the yobs and slobs that comprised their new neighbourhood, there was still that same spark of greatness lurking beneath the surface. The intelligence and intensity that she had fallen in love with never faded. He was still the same man, and the same as always. She couldn't get him to do what she wanted, even when it was what was best for him.

John's interest in her was waning. Their sex life had slowed to a stuttering halt despite his suddenly renewed interest in it. Unlike many men, he did not take this abrupt lack of interest as an insult. Rather, he took it as a sign that he needed to find his entertainment elsewhere.

Making friends always came easy to John; finding lovers didn't come much harder. Suzanne Allen was widely known to be sexually promiscuous, and despite her age and relative lack of appeal to John, she was what he considered to be a sure thing. They began having sex irregularly during the following couple of years, with his visits to her property easily masked by the presence of his 'buddy' Ray living in her back garden. No matter what was going on, she would reliably drop everything and drop her pants the moment that he walked in the door. Given her perpetual state of unemployment, it wasn't often that she had anything else going on anyway, but on the rare occasion that she was babysitting her two grandsons, she would send them out to play in the back garden, on the assumption that Ray would come charging out the way that he always did if there was any sign of trouble.

There was not even the slightest sense of equality in the relationship, and despite his repeatedly stated lack of attraction to the older woman, he enjoyed their dynamic. She did whatever he wanted whenever he wanted it, and he looked on with dispassionate boredom more often than not, making her degrade herself in new and inventive ways, just because he could. She was available for his use, so he used her, and no matter how emotionally attached she was to him, he didn't ever fear that she was going to act out and disrupt his marriage. She was too used to being the other woman, accepting whatever scraps of attention were given to her, and he was too certain of his utter dominance over her.

And so, a year passed, with nothing much changing at all. John settled more into his life on the fringes; his new friends settled into their roles as subservient to him. He began killing animals again, skinning them alive or burning them to death, just for the amusement that it brought him.

It wasn't enough, of course. Nothing was ever enough.

He met Elizabeth Harvey at one of the regular house parties that popped up in the neighbourhood, and the two of them hit it off. She was newly divorced and damaged enough by her previous relationship to view an affair with John Bunting as a romantic proposition. She also had children in tow, though that was less than immediately apparent to John when they met.

While his affair with Suzanne was all about scratching an itch and feeling powerful, in Elizabeth, he saw a second chance at romance in his life. He courted her as if she were a potential girlfriend, took her out on what passed for dates in Salisbury North, and even introduced himself to the one teen son that she'd managed to extract from the mess of her previous relationship.

Until the moment that he met young James Vlassakis, Elizabeth was convinced that John was a flight risk. That at a moment's notice, he might turn tail and abandon her. Go running back to his wife with his tail between his legs. This was the opposite direction to the one in which John took off at speed.

James, known by almost everyone as Jamie, was a troubled boy. Damaged in ways that even his mother had not been able to decipher by the abuse that he had suffered at the hands of his father and stepbrother while he lived under their roof. At a glance, John could see that damage. He could tell where all the rage and confusion bubbling up inside of Jamie was coming from. It was like looking into his past. A haunted reflection of what he could have become if he hadn't found his lethal outlet for all the loathing that Jamie had turned inward.

John had a child, somewhere out there in the world, but he would never know that child. Never spend time with it. Never raise it or shape it or share what he had learned from his own experiences. There was a hole in the centre of his heart in the shape of the baby that had been snatched away from him, and Jamie fit it almost perfectly.

That brief meeting changed the trajectory of all their lives. John's state of dispassionate observation was disrupted. He wanted, and he loathed himself for the weakness of that wanting. The boy, as much as the second chances that the mother represented, drew him in, and before a year was out, he was making something of an indecent proposal to her. He wanted her and her son to come and live with him.

He had not informed his wife of this fact. Throughout the year-long courtship of Elizabeth and Jamie, she had become aware that he was having an affair, but she could not conceive of any way to confront him about it that wouldn't end in her feeling like an even bigger fool than she already did. When she knew that the other woman was going to be at a social event, she'd mysteriously develop a headache and stay home. When John spoke about Elizabeth, or more frequently Jamie, she would grit her teeth and pretend that they were just friends. He didn't go out of his way to rub her face in the infidelity, but neither did he make any attempt to hide things from her. The grapevine in their little slice of heaven was far too deeply rooted for that. She knew that he was sleeping with another woman. She could almost have tolerated that. What really hurt was that he seemed to be entirely replacing her in his affections with this other woman.

If she'd been left with even a grain of self-respect by the time that Elizabeth and Jamie showed up in a moving van, then she would have walked out then and there, but John had worn her down so far that she looked at what was happening and she truly believed that it was her fault. She wasn't keeping John satisfied. She wasn't giving him what he wanted out of life. She'd been so focused on trying to push him back onto the path that she wanted for him that she'd ended up pushing him away, and now she was paying the price for all those long, cold nights apart.

Yet for all of the inherent cruelty in moving his mistress into their home and sharing a bed under the same roof as her, John didn't seem to be vindictive. He was still as circumspect as he could be about the relationship; he never forced any confrontation. It was almost as if he expected them to just grow used to each other. To become comfortable with this polygamy in everything but name.

Veronica could not make herself comfortable with it. She could not reconcile the love that she felt for her husband with the way that he treated her. While they were not officially separated or divorced, she would go to stay with her family for weeks and sometimes months at a time. Often without warning. If John was sorry to see her go, he never let it slip.

By the time that Elizabeth Harvey and her son had been living there for a year, Veronica had stopped coming back for more suffering. That suited John just fine. Their relationship had been entirely too equitable for his tastes. Elizabeth came to him already prepared to be servile and thankful for the affection that he showed her. Her previous marriage had shown her just how badly relationships could go, and that made John seem like a living saint by comparison. The fact that he would go so far above and beyond what was asked of him when it came to Jamie just solidified her abject devotion to him. He could have murdered a man in front of her eyes, and she still would have considered it justified. He could have done anything, and she would have absolved him. If Veronica had been a leash, holding him back, then Elizabeth was a whip, driving John on to even greater depths of depravity.

Nineteen ninety-five was a very good year for John. His stepson Jamie moved in with them on a permanent basis after the latest round of fights with his biological father, and the time for the boy's indoctrination into John's personal school of trauma management began soon after.

Jamie had already confided in John more than he ever had his own mother or any of the friends that he'd managed to cling to through the years. He loved John like the father that he'd never had. It was like the relationship that John had been trying to cultivate with Robert with some gasoline tossed on top for good measure.

It started with dogs and cats. John taught the boy how to hunt them, how to trick them into following after him without being seen. If they'd lived out in the country, maybe their attention might have been turned to other animals, but in suburbia, they made do with what was available. It was all just practice. John was too old to go hustling for business around the gay clubs in Adelaide with any hope of success. If he wanted to get back into the gay-bashing and mugging business, he needed somebody to serve as bait. And if he wanted to escalate the violence – as he so desperately wanted to do – then he would need to ensure that the boy he used for bait would not only accept it, but would also be complicit in it.

He skinned a cat alive in front of the boy. Let him hear the screams, see the blood and the viscera spilling out without the skin to contain it. The noises that the cat made were horrific. Nightmarish sounds that haunted Jamie's dreams. But he didn't look away. He didn't flinch. The thought of letting John down was worse than watching an animal get tortured to death.

Next time, Jamie joined in. He didn't make any of the difficult cuts on the stray dog – John didn't want to risk him hurting himself – but he did get to pin the animal down by the neck so that it couldn't bite. He got to feel every whimper, whine, and wail vibrating against the palm of his hand. He got to feel the sudden slick as blood rushed to escape the parted skin and fur. He got to feel it all, right up until the moment that the living body stopped living, and the flesh grew cold. John's hands were busy, but his eyes never left the boy's face. This was a more dangerous moment than murdering a man in cold blood in his own living room. Back then, he knew how every one of the pieces on the board was going to move. Now he was dealing with an unknown variable. Jamie performed admirably. Pleasing his new father figure in ways that he could not have even known.

John did not force the boy to participate in the killings. He even went out of his way to perform a few when the boy couldn't have known what was going on so that the kid didn't feel like the older man was missing out on his account if he did decide not to join in. Once again, Jamie performed beyond all of John's wildest expectations, even acting irritated with John when he did not invite him along for the hunt.

The next step would be the most difficult. He knew that, in theory, both Elizabeth and Jamie were committed to his fight, but he needed to know for certain that they were willing to go the necessary distance when the time came. He needed an opportunity to introduce them to the idea that killing human beings was not only acceptable, but normal. A part of their everyday life. What luck, then, that the body of Clinton Trezise had just been uncovered.

The police had no leads. They were appealing to the public for any information about the death. It took them weeks from the discovery of the body in its shallow grave to the point where they could even identify the victim, thanks to the thorough job John had done shattering the pieces of the face that could be used for dental record verification. Even when the man's name became public knowledge, nobody could work out what had happened. Clinton had been a solitary man with a limited circle of friends, none of whom had reported him missing. Even his family hadn't known that he was absent, because he'd cut off all contact with them years before. If the corpse had not been found, nobody would have even noticed that Clinton was gone. The perfect victim.

The problems of his solitary life and absent criminal record were perpetuated throughout the investigation. Nobody knew why anybody might have wanted to hurt Clinton. If it was true that he had been some sort of child molester, then there would have been families of his victims to serve as viable suspects, but as Clinton had essentially done no wrong to anyone, there was no motive. Passing mention was made in the news reports of the sum of money that had accrued in the form of benefits cheques in his abandoned apartment, but even that did nothing to provide clarity. If he'd been killed for money, those cheques would have been the incentive.

Because John had killed for no rational reason, his crime was impossible to understand.

It was during one of the segments of Australia's Most Wanted when John leaned over to Jamie on the other side of his mother on the sofa and said, 'I did that one. Paedo.'

There was another one of those long moments when John waited for the dice to fall as they may. When he had even odds of the whole situation suddenly exploding out of his control or of the reality that he was insisting upon asserting itself. It stretched on for a minute before Elizabeth mumbled, awe-struck. 'Good on you.'

'Can't have them running around touching kids, can I? Not when all it takes is a good whack to stop 'em. The police knew about him and they did nothing. Everyone around here knew what he was up to. They all knew, and they just let it happen. I didn't let it happen. I wouldn't ever let somebody hurt kids.'

He made meaningful eye contact with Jamie as he said it. He knew that the boy had been sexually abused. He recognised the unique scars that it left on a boy's psyche to be used like that. The only question was whether he was getting through to Jamie, even through that thick layer of scar tissue. Was his message being heard? Jamie gave him a terse nod. 'Good on you, John.'

John finally had the perfect fighting unit prepared for his holy war on paedophiles. Now all that he needed was a fresh pool of victims.

Luckily, he already had a source of intelligence primed and ready to spill his guts about every other sex offender that he'd ever met. Barry Lane.

With Veronica gone, John was now free to share the bed of Elizabeth, leaving a spare room in the house, the wall of which soon became dominated by what has since been called a rock spider wall.

Scraps of paper with names, dates, addresses, phone numbers. Relationships and connections between them displayed with threads of wool stuck in place with pins. Each of the names slowly and carefully extracted from Barry and the general hubbub of rumour. The men that John had decided were gay and/or paedophiles – terms that he considered to be synonymous. There was no attempt to gather evidence or to build a case against any of these men. John did not work for the police; he did not care about seeing them tried for their crimes. He served a higher purpose than the laws of man. He served righteous vengeance.

As it turned out, righteous vengeance wasn't all that bothered about whether the victims of the violence being doled out in its name were actually guilty of the things that they were being accused of. John was very much of the opinion that the death of a few suspicious bystanders was a small price to pay in exchange for ridding the world of this evil.

When he felt his rage rising, he would go into the spare room and make some calls, hurling abuse and accusations at whichever man on the board was his prime target of the day. Insinuating that he had evidence. Suggesting that they kill themselves rather than suffer the shame and indignity that was soon going to be heaped on them when he turned them in to the police. Some of them contacted the police to discuss the harassment and found themselves under investigation for the very things that they were being wrongly accused of. The smart ones kept quiet. An accusation like this, even if it were proven untrue beyond any shadow of a doubt, would still stain a man's reputation for the rest of his life. But some of the accused didn't have the benefit of that sort of intelligence to protect them.

One day, Suzanne Allen's grandkids came barrelling back into the house from the garden, screaming and feigning vomiting after Ray had come out of his caravan with no trousers on.

Ray was in the habit of rushing outside whenever he heard a noise. This was likely to be far from the first time that he had heard a noise and rushed out without fully dressing himself, but it was the first time that he had charged out, screaming threats, only to discover two young boys eye level to his crotch.

The kids were upset. Their mother was enraged. It was the talk of the whole neighbourhood, that dumb old Ray had finally shown his true colours and exposed himself to some poor unsuspecting kids. By the time that it passed along the grapevine to Barry's ears, the story had already transformed into the mentally disabled man attempting to force himself on the boys. It was in much the same state of mangling when it came separately to John.

Of course, John already had Ray up on his board as a suspect, thanks to his prior association with Barry, and he had a more direct source of intelligence relating to what had happened in Allen's backyard than waiting for Barry to come crawling around, trying to put his own spin on things.

In John's mind, if not in reality, Barry and Ray had been an on-and-off item throughout the years. Now that he had successfully wrested Robert away from the older man, John suspected that Barry had gone back to using Ray for his perverse sexual pleasure in much the same way that Suzanne Allen sometimes did.

This meant that any intelligence Barry provided would be tainted. It didn't seem to cross John's mind that there was any conflict of interest when it came to information coming from Suzanne on that same note. So long as information supported his worldview and, more specifically, encouraged him to acts of violence, he would believe in it no matter how much evidence later turned up to the contrary.

A short visit with Suzanne, which coincidentally ended in sex, provided John with all the information that he wanted to hear. According to what he had worked out of Suzanne, Ray had attempted to proposition the boys. He was a grown man exposing himself to minors. Even if he lacked the mental capacity to understand what that meant, that was tantamount to forcing himself on them, and it should be punished as such.

Suzanne, in her wrath, did not even stop to consider the significance of telling John the altered version of events. She wanted some petty revenge on Ray for what he'd done and the chewing out that she'd received from her daughter for letting the boys get into such a dangerous situation. With her spite, she unknowingly signed the man's death warrant.

With Barry compromised, John narrowed down his potential soldiers in the coming conflict to himself, Robert, Jamie and, unexpectedly, Elizabeth.

John and Robert entered the caravan at the back of the property under cover of darkness after John had made an additional visit to Suzanne, just to ensure that she slept right through anything that might be overheard in her backyard over the coming hours.

Ray was startled at their sudden appearance, but not panicked. They were his friends after all. People that came into his caravan quite regularly and that he knew could be trusted.

When they hauled him out of bed, he mostly thought that they were playing a game and rough-housing with him as they had in the past. When they dragged him silently through the back gardens along to John's house, he was caught up in the excitement. He was dangling between them laughing all the way. They were dragging him by the arms, but he was pumping his legs along with them to get to where they were going. He was marching to his own death with a blank smile on his face.

They didn't let go of him even when they were in the house and out of sight. They didn't let go of him as they hauled him through to the bathroom. All the way, he was laughing along, thinking it was all a game, even when the men had dead blank expressions on their faces.

He didn't understand what was happening, even as the garotte of rope was looped around his neck and tightened with a twist of a tire iron. The strength left his body with the flow of blood to his brain reduced. The world went grey and hazy.

When John went away and came back with a bat, he didn't understand. His body seemed to grasp it, though. It bucked and pulled, and John bellowed at the others to hold him down. Taking careful aim, he then slammed the blunt end of the cricket bat into Ray's crotch. The pain was not instant, and it had to cut through the haze of confusion, but when it arrived, he let out a screech that it took another full turn of the tire iron to cut off. 'Not going to be fucking any more kids with that, are you?'

John struck again and again. Some thrusts bounced off Ray's flopping thighs. Others hammered home again and again until his genitals were ripped almost entirely off his body, his testicles reduced to paste. The pain burned through it all, a bright white flame in a world full of dull grey static. Ray still tried to cry out. Sobbing and begging silently. Trying to tell them that he'd never done anything. Even if the words had made it out, nobody would have believed them. John said he was a paedophile. That meant he was a paedophile.

He handed the bat off to Jamie, and all it took was one nod of encouragement before the boy started swinging. Taking a few wild whacks at the man before falling into the same rhythm that John had used. Short abrupt thrusts, hitting Ray in the gut for the most part. Sometimes drifting down to the bloody mess between his legs. 'Never doing it again. Never again.'

Elizabeth did not have the visceral hatred for paedophiles that John and her son had cultivated through their personal experiences, but she had lived a long life at the mercy of men just like Ray. Blank-eyed drooling morons who did whatever they wanted to get their satisfaction, no matter who got hurt. More dangerous still, she was a mother. The protective instincts that motherhood brought out in her had not faded as her son grew older. Every day, she could see him suffering, without ever knowing why. Every day, she knew that he was in pain, but was too afraid to even ask him why for fear of breaking down the dam holding all his darker experiences at bay.

All that she knew was that punishing this monstrous paedophile was the only thing that she had ever seen granting her son some reprieve from the suffering that plagued his every waking moment. She would not stop that. Not for a man like Ray. Not for anything. There were plenty of tools laying on the bathroom floor, leftovers from John's various forays into manual labour. She started working over Ray's legs with a socket wrench.

It took John back for a moment, then he started cheering her on the same way he had Jamie. It was completely unexpected. He'd expected her to stand there and watch. To be complicit without having to get her hands dirty. He could never have dreamed that she'd dive right in and start swinging.

Through the oxygen deprivation, it was hard to say how much of the violence was even making it to Ray's brain. He was still making pained sounds, certainly, and the actual sight of blood spreading beneath his clothes seemed to be enough to excite John and his soldiers in this holy war, even if the man couldn't feel it. Much like everything else in John's life, it didn't matter what the truth was. It didn't matter if the man was suffering, so long as it looked to John like he was suffering. It didn't matter if the man was guilty, so long as it looked to John like he was guilty.

In the mad drag through the back yards to the house, one of Ray's shoes had fallen off, and the sight of toes curling and flexing to the pain gave John an idea. He took a pair of pliers and clamped them down onto Ray's big toe, squeezing with all of his strength until the nail detached and the flesh was little more than pulp. It was the only truly exposed injury. The only place where they could see the blood of their victim flowing. For John, it was finally enough.

After a half-hour of this prolonged and haphazard torture, John gave Robert a nod, and he made one final rotation of the tire iron behind Ray's head, cutting the rope right into the man's skin and robbing him of whatever residual air he was still managing to drag in. He could have died that moment or ten minutes later and nobody in the room would have known one way or the other. Ray was still from the moment that the last rotation was made.

After the initial frenzy of violence on the disabled man's sexual organs, John had hung back and let the others work, conserving his energy for the work that was still to be done that night.

In the back garden of their home, he and Jamie dug a grave. It was slow work. Both men were exhausted after the excitement earlier on. Jamie genuinely would have preferred to fall into his bed and the welcome oblivion that was awaiting him there, but John still considered the boy to be in the final stages of his training. He wanted to see which way the kid was going to jump after he'd finally graduated to murder.

John's hands moved through the motions. His shoulders clenched. The spade bit soil. But through it all, his eyes were on Jamie. To anyone else, the boy would have been as inscrutable as ever, but John knew him. He knew the maze of trauma that the boy was walking, and he needed to know that they were both going to come out in the same place.

He need not have worried. All the groundwork that he'd laid with the boy over the past few months had prepared Jamie perfectly for his moment of truth. It was there in the flush of the boy's cheeks. The spring in his step. There was no doubt or regret in the boy, and when they finally dragged the corpse out, wrapped in the shower curtain, and deposited it into the ground, Jamie spat right down into Ray's grave.

John gave him an approving nod, then let the boy off to sleep. Robert came out and picked up the shovel, assuming his place by John's side once more now that his replacement in the other man's affections seemed to be done with.

In the days that followed, they cleaned out Ray's caravan. Over the time that they'd known each other, Ray had borrowed most of the things that he owned from the others. Clearing out his belongings ended up being mostly acts of repatriation. The few things that were genuinely Ray's were consigned to the garbage dump.

Suzanne had no complaints about the sudden absence of her tenant, but she wasn't happy when John and the others arranged for the caravan to vanish. In the garden of a friend's house over in Elizabeth, the men worked on it like a hobby whenever they were in the mood, stripping off the original paint and re-spraying it in different colours. Giving the old hunk of metal a full overhaul until it could be sold for almost as much as a new one just a couple of months later. Through the back pages of the local papers, it was moved along, and the takings were passed along to Suzanne, both as hush money and to ease the passing of her renter.

She never spoke to John about what had happened. She never asked any questions, though it seems likely she thought that the man had been driven off with threats rather than facing the far more permanent fate that John had bestowed upon him. By the time the seasons changed, it was as though Ray had never even existed. He had nobody who missed him. He had nobody looking for him. He was the perfect victim.

It only made John hungry for more.

Killing for a Living

Ray's murder had been the perfect crime from John's perspective, while the death of Clinton Trezise had lacked one of the components that had made John's earlier crimes sustainable as a long-term career. Ray's murder had provided him with monetary compensation for the efforts involved.

Ray had been as gullible and simple a mark as anyone John had ever met in his life. When they'd first crossed paths, it had been John that taught the man about all of the benefits that he was entitled to from the government and ensured that he would be able to pay both his rent and for his share of the beers when they all hung out. He knew every detail of Ray's claim, and that his cheques were being delivered to the house of Suzanne.

John visited her frequently in the days after Ray's mysterious disappearance to pump her for information, sidestepping around any conversation about Ray himself while still digging for the details he required to get his hands on the money. It was pretty close to the ideal situation for John. The money was already coming to somebody that he had complete control over, so all that he had to do was swing by and collect it. The last thing that he had wanted to do was send in a request for a change of address, not when it might attract official attention to Ray. Whether he chose to share a cut with Suzanne to ensure her compliance and complicity is unclear. She certainly didn't seem to struggle more financially after Ray's disappearance, but given the high-tension nature of her sexual relationship with John, it was entirely plausible that providing for her financially might have weakened his hold over her. Regardless, she never contacted the police, or anyone else.

With an additional stream of income, and his base of followers solidly established, John made his next move, relocating to the peaceful town of Murray Bridge, about seventy miles east of Adelaide. For their money, he and Elizabeth were able to get a larger house, with more ground outside. Ground that didn't have a corpse buried in it.

The same intelligence that made John into a formidable ringleader for his little gang also rendered him susceptible to overthinking. There was too much evidence tying him to the death of Ray – all it would take would be one over-eager social worker poking around and his whole world might fall apart. That was why he'd sold off the caravan, that was why he'd moved out of town. The distance made him feel safer.

John still frequently visited his old friends in Adelaide, of course. A little distance wasn't going to get in the way of those relationships, or his stops by Suzanne's house to pick up his cheques.

Change was afoot in Salisbury North everywhere that the eye turned. Mark Haydon, one of John's longest-standing supporters, had fallen in love and married a woman named Elizabeth. A woman who was less than fond of John and the hold that he seemed to have over her husband. She opposed John at every turn, from something as simple as asking Mark around to have a drink, to the more complex criminal enterprises that he was funnelling money to his old buddy to perform. What's more, she showed him none of the respect that he was accustomed to receiving from women. She even made jokes at his expense.

John was not accustomed to being mocked. He had fled halfway across the continent to get away from people with meaningful smirks like Elizabeth had splattered across her face. She could not have made a more dangerous enemy for herself.

When confronted with a problem that he could not address directly, John went around it. He befriended Elizabeth's sister, Jodie, who seemed to be as susceptible to his charms as any other woman. He befriended her disabled nephew, Fred Brooks. He sought out any hint of vulnerability in her social circles, and he burrowed in until he was so entangled, not only in Mark's life, but in Elizabeth's, that getting him out might tear the whole thing apart.

Even still, he wasn't content. In private, away from Mark, he would rant and rage about the harridan who had taken one of his best mates away from him. The situation worsened. Just as John had moved away from his old stomping ground, so did Mark and Elizabeth, relocating to a nicer suburb of Adelaide. This removed the base of operations that John had always assumed would remain available to him within Salisbury North.

With Mark out of the picture, John fell back on Suzanne more and more frequently. The more time that they spent together, the more pronounced the tensions in their relationship became, until finally, it seemed the whole arrangement between them might come apart at the seams.

There are two versions of what happened next, the one widely accepted by those who knew John, and the version that could be legally proven in the years to come. In the unprovable version, John and Suzanne fell out, and she threatened to contact the police with information about the disappearance of Ray, resulting in her murder. In the other version, John arrived at Suzanne's home, let himself in as usual, and discovered her already dead on the bed, having expired from one of her many health issues.

What followed afterwards is the same in both versions. Without Suzanne, John would lose access to Ray's money. He was also sharply aware of the large amount of money that she regularly received in government bursaries. An opportunity to secure both sets of money had just presented itself. All that was required was that nobody learn about Suzanne's death.

With clinical precision, John dismembered her body and wrapped the parts in plastic bags. Waiting until nightfall, he strolled along through the shared back gardens to the currently unlet house where he used to live, opened up Ray's grave, and added the bags one by one before covering the whole thing up again. Her rent would continue to be paid directly by the government. Her constant fighting with family members had left her isolated. The only thing that would pile up in her absence was mail, and John was more than happy to handle that on his frequent visits.

More money presented more opportunities, but with the slight improvement to their living situation, John was essentially satisfied. He didn't need more luxury to be content, and while he dispensed money freely to his companions in crime, they didn't require much, either.

The money had to serve a purpose. It couldn't just sit and accrue interest or eventually the government might take notice and cut off the various benefits that John was claiming for himself. What John needed – what he really needed – was a way to get away with murder. Without that, all of the money was worthless. It obsessed him. All of the intellect that he was so proud of was twisted to focus on that one problem. He had the resources, all he needed was the solution.

Mark Haydon became that solution. Now that he was no longer living in such close proximity with the rest of them, there was no tie between him and the rest of the conspirators. He could be the legal 'front' to all of their illegal activities. John began funnelling more and more money to the man, making quiet arrangements when they got together for a beer. None of it local. None of it obvious. Just little pieces of the bigger picture, scattered all around South Australia. A purchase here. A rental property there.

Snowtown was an agricultural community on the decline, a place drifting further and further from its long-forgotten dreams of being a city and now shrinking towards a ghost town. A town so desolate that even the bank on the main street had closed down, forcing the locals to trek for miles to Kadina or Crystal Brook if they wanted to deposit a cheque.

It was the building that once held the bank that drew Mark and John's attention. It was an unassuming building, built to purpose, so utterly useless to any other investors looking to open a store up in the town. The rent was not low, by any stretch of the imagination, but it was low enough that the funds collected from Ray and Suzanne's benefits easily covered it. Inside it was a time capsule of stuffy late-eighties corporate Australia, at least on the surface. John didn't give a damn about the surface. What he wanted were the vaults. Down beneath the level of the street were cold concrete chambers that could be sealed against the outside world.

His obsession with capture was always focused on the discovery of the bodies. As long as the bodies existed, John felt certain that they would provide all the evidence required to see him jailed, but by extension, if he could dispose of them entirely, he became untouchable. No body, no crime.

His old interest in chemistry merged with his obsession with being the smartest one in the room. He purchased the components for powerful acids from different chemical supply companies, using different members of his team to make each batch and spacing them out across different towns.

Down in the vaults, he put it all together. Great plastic barrels were filled up halfway with acid and carefully sealed, everything calculated mentally to old memorized formulas and organised to John's specifications. There were dozens of those barrels down in the vaults. Enough for him to wage his war on the paedophiles for years without pause.

As if to prove John's fears right, the police came knocking at his door in Murray Bridge before he could go looking for one.

In an instant, he was ready to fight them off, to burn down the house, to do whatever he had to do to escape prison. He'd heard all about prison. What happened to attractive men there. If there was a hell, that was it for John. To be powerless and passed around. He'd rather die than suffer that. He'd rather kill everyone on the planet than suffer that. Yet despite that instant readiness to fight or flee, he spoke softly and calmly to the officers, giving no hint that there was anything wrong. If he could talk his way out of a problem, he was happy to do so. Whatever worked, he would do.

As it turned out, the police were making simple enquiries about some discrepancies regarding Suzanne Allen's cheques. One had been cashed in Murray Bridge, rather than Adelaide where they were usually deposited, and the address written on the back of the cheque was his. Such a simple mistake when he was depositing the stacks of cheques that he received, scribbling the wrong details on the wrong bit of paper, but it almost brought the whole enterprise tumbling down. The police departed after he told them that Suzanne Allen was a close personal friend and he helped her out with her finances. There was no question about whether Suzanne was still alive. No question about how she was receiving the money from the cheques that he cashed for her. If there was no complaint brought to their attention, then this wasn't a matter for the police. People could do whatever they wanted with their own money.

None of this dissuaded John from his course. If anything, it just proved to him once more that he was smarter than the police, smarter than the system, smarter than everyone. He was already getting away with murder on at least two counts, and the police weren't even asking about them. What couldn't he get away with?

His harassment of people on his rock-spider wall escalated. Not only did he ring them up at all hours of the night to make his baseless claims, but he also began organizing outings for his little gang, visiting the homes of his potential targets, breaking in and vandalizing the place. None of the victims reported the break-ins to the police. Not when the same vile accusations about them had been spray-painted across their walls for anyone to see.

Without any leads solid enough to prompt action, John went to Barry for fresh intelligence, as he always did, and came away with a list of fresh paedophiles that mysteriously coincided with whoever the old cross-dresser had a personal grudge against in any given week. This time, the target was Michael 'Michele' Gardiner.

Robert Wagner only had limited contact with Barry now that he was an adult and John had so carefully extracted him from their pseudo-romantic entanglement, yet the last time that the two of them had spoken, all Robert had on his mind was Michael Gardiner. The boy was an openly gay teenager living on his own and turning heads with exactly the same flamboyant behaviour that Barry used to favour before he'd adopted his new, more quiet lifestyle. Robert seethed every time that he saw him, but Barry suspected that a tumultuous relationship might be the end result of the obsession, just as the boy had initially been repulsed and drawn to him in equal measure. 'Michele' was a younger, better-looking version of Barry, and Barry just couldn't stand it. He fed the boy to John and his gang without a second thought.

Further scouting and research revealed all the details that John needed to know. The boy was isolated from his family, thanks to the revelation of his sexuality, living alone in the rented room of a middle-aged woman who treated him more like a friend than a surrogate child. She'd suffered bad luck with previous tenants vanishing in the dead of night and leaving her in the lurch. It was an ideal setup as far as John was concerned. Intercepting his mail provided confirmation that Michael was living off benefit payments and sealed his fate.

The gang abducted him from the house where he was staying, with Robert taking a lead role in the acts of casual violence now that he had the opportunity. Every time that he looked at Michael, he saw the grown man who'd abused him as a young teenager. The effeminate Barry had warped his understanding of right and wrong until he believed that they were in love. Robert couldn't undo the past, but he could stop it from repeating. He could keep this Barry from abusing whichever kid came along, lost and confused.

It didn't even cross Robert's mind that Michael was nothing like Barry and considerably more like him, barely more than a child, on the run from a family that hated him, in a desperate situation about to be made much worse by grown men who cared more about getting what they wanted than the damage it would do.

They stole as much of Michael's property as they could carry on the way out of the house before throwing him into the backseat of Mark's car and heading for Snowtown. Trying to make it look like he had abandoned his home the same way that the previous tenants had. His landlady didn't believe it for a moment. She reached out to Michael's friends, to the police, to anyone who would listen. Nobody would listen.

In Snowtown, in the dedicated space that John had set aside for it, Michael suffered. In addition to the beatings that their previous victims had to live through, John and the rest of his cabal electrocuted Michael, attaching crocodile clips to his flesh and wires to a car battery. Eventually, when the Live album that John had put on the boombox was coming to an end, he was the one to choke the life out of Michael. Not because he had any greater desire to do it than any of the others, but because he'd seen the hunger for it in Robert's eyes, and he needed to assert control. They had to be loyal to him, not to the mission, not to the pleasure of the kill, to him and only him. And if that meant taking the pleasure of the kill from them, then that was what he would do. Only through him were they allowed to experience this savage joy. Only through him did the money flow. He needed, pathologically needed, to be at the centre of this whole enterprise, and if he couldn't have that, then nobody got what they wanted out of it.

With Gardiner dead, they pushed him down into one of the acid barrels and left him to dissolve, shifting their attention from the fun part of the murder to the part that was all business.

John went through the boy's belongings so that he could find his identification, the only thing required for them to go on intercepting and cashing the boy's benefits cheques. His wallet was not there. John immediately flew into a rage, hauling all of the belongings that they'd seized alongside the boy into the bank and tearing through them, often literally, in search of the wallet. It was not there. They'd left it behind in the house. The house that Michael's suspicious landlady had now returned to. They had all of the intelligence that they needed on him, but nothing on her. If they killed her, she could bring the whole conspiracy crashing down around their ears. They needed to get the wallet out of her house.

Two days after Michael's disappearance, they scoped out his old room and found that it had been cleaned out and tidied up. Breaking and entering was no longer a viable option. If the wallet had been in that room, then the landlady was now in possession of it, and there was no way to know where she would have put it. They needed to convince her to hand it over, retrieving it from wherever it had been hidden as was necessary.

None of the men were going to pass for Michael. None of them could pass as one of his social circle, either. Direct contact of any kind would have been an intolerable risk anyway. They needed a pliable third party to do their dirty work.

It was time for John to flex his control over the network of people that he'd built up around himself, to find someone disposable yet viable for this operation.

Fred Brooks, the mentally disabled son of Mark Haydon's wife's sister, was the perfect tool for the job. Obedient to any authority figure, with a childish enough voice to sound like one of Michael's little gay friends, John had him on the phone to

Michael's landlady within twenty-four hours of them scouting out the victim's room and finding it clean.

The story was simple enough for even Fred to remember. He was a friend of Michael's. Michael had moved to a new city with other friends. Michael needed his wallet back so he could get his benefits moved with him. It was all very reasonable. Except for the fact that it was so wildly out of character for Michael that the landlady couldn't believe a word of it. She insisted on speaking to Michael. Insisted that if Michael really wanted his wallet back, then he would contact her directly. That she wasn't angry about him leaving, but she wasn't going to hand off his wallet to somebody that she'd never met.

John was silently fuming, listening in on the call. He'd hoped that the woman would be angry enough to wash her hands of Michael as quickly as possible, but she wasn't playing along to his script. Over the course of a week, they tried repeatedly with the same spiel, each time making it sound like Michael's situation was dire and he needed access to his funds. The landlady even offered a meetup with Michael himself to pass over the wallet, but even though the others were chomping at the bit to simply mug this woman for the wallet, John wasn't biting on that bait. It felt too much like the traps that he'd used to set up for potential victims.

He was correct in his assessment. From the outset, the landlady had been in contact with the police about the disappearance of the boy, and the repeated calls demanding his wallet had only enhanced her sense that something was wrong. There was no reason that Michael could not call her. She had fully intended on bringing the police along for this 'meetup' to hand over the wallet.

In the end, the gang had to leave the money on the table. The first kill that John had felt truly satisfied with now had a bitter aftertaste. Their operation had been as close to flawless as he could conceive of, striking at a target with no personal connection to any of them, and still somehow his people had failed him at this critical juncture.

Traitors to the Cause

In the aftermath of Michael's disappearance, it became immediately apparent to Barry Lane that his days were numbered. He knew that John had only kept him around for his information, and now that he had seen the result of handing out that information, he didn't think that he could stomach dispensing any more. In his bitterness about his failed relationship with Wagner, he had lost sight of the reality that he was trapped in. There was a killer on his doorstep, and he had no means to protect himself without handing himself in to the police, where John would likely be hailed as a hero and Barry suffer more of the same discrimination and indignities that he'd been through the last time he was in prison.

He was terrified and, above all, he was tired of facing his problems alone. It had been a long time since he'd been in anything resembling a relationship, since John had taken even the small comfort of a lover in his bed away from him.

Thomas Trevilyan seemed to come out of nowhere to solve all of Barry's problems. The man had lived in the neighbourhood for a few years without ever crossing Barry's path, in no small part because the older man believed that the gentleman marching vigorously around in full military camouflage might not have taken to an old transvestite drooling over him. As it turned out, his preconceptions were incorrect.

Trevilyan suffered from a variety of mental illnesses that had rendered him unfit for military service, but that had not prevented his childhood obsession from continuing to dominate his life. He dressed entirely in army surplus, carried a knife, travelled great distances on foot and worked out every hour that the day gave him. He was obsessed with reaching peak combat fitness, honing his skills as an unofficial soldier.

Eventually, out of boredom as much as anything else, Barry invited him into his back garden for a drink during the hot summer of 1997 when he spotted him marching around the backstreets behind his house.

The two men hit it off. Barry was suitably impressed with Thomas's physical fitness, and Thomas greatly enjoyed being treated like a human being rather than some sort of bizarre imposition. The turning point between friendship and romance came a little later but was soon followed up by Trevilyan moving into Barry's house with him as a live-in husband and unofficial bodyguard. A kept man.

It is unclear whether it was Trevilyan's inherent paranoia or the stories that Barry told him that resulted in his rushing out of the house brandishing a knife every time there was a noise outside, but it seems likely to have been a pre-existing condition, given how many of his neighbours over the past few years reported seeing him darting in and out of his flat at all hours of the day and night.

With Trevilyan in place to protect him, Barry finally felt safe enough to start talking about his experiences with John and the rest of the gang, mentioning not only the recent disappearance of young Michael Gardiner but the unsolved murder of Clinton Trezise. News did not reach the police, but rumours did begin to circulate in the neighbourhood, potentially poisoning the potential victim pool and preventing John from repeating his move against Michael Gardiner on any of the other targets he'd earmarked.

Needless to say, John was enraged when word reached him. He had been absolutely certain of his control over Barry after the Trezise killing. Absolutely positive that the man would never dare to move against him, but now he discovered that time and distance had numbed his effect to such a degree that he was now in danger. Barry might not have been able to approach the police directly with information, but if rumours found their way to the wrong detective's ears, then the comfortable life that John had constructed for himself could fall apart all too quickly.

So it was that John and Barry's old flame, Robert Wagner, showed up on his doorstep shortly after nightfall in October with a six-pack of beer to share with the intention of getting to the bottom of all this rumour spreading nonsense. He welcomed them in and introduced them to Thomas, even though they'd met plenty of times before throughout the years. It seemed to bring the other two men up short, finding Thomas waiting there in the living room, larger than life.

As they talked, Barry was quite candid about who he had told what to. He was no fool, putting his neck on the line, but he also wasn't just going to sit back and let John and his little gang murder people for pleasure or profit. As he spoke, Thomas drifted over to stand behind him, looming over the whole living room and making his bulk apparent in case the visitors happened to forget it.

At the end of his little speech about how despicable they were, Barry looked to John and asked him plainly, 'Anything else?'

John shook his head. Barry had already told him everything that he wanted to know. He looked up at Thomas and gave him the nod that they'd agreed on.

Barry didn't even know what was happening as Thomas's big hands clamped around his throat and dragged him out of the chair, hauling him through to the bathroom. Barry was desperately trying to call for help and finding that he couldn't get enough breath to make anything more than a strangled squeak. He faded in and out of consciousness until he resurfaced in the bathtub, cradled and pinned safely in Thomas's arms as he'd been so many nights before. At the foot of the tub, John was standing grinning with a pair of pliers in his hands. 'Here's how it is going to go. You're going to say what I want, when I want. Or I'm going to start crushing toes. Got it?'

Barry got it.

The house phone was dragged through and the earpiece placed carefully against the side of Barry's head as Thomas recited the only phone number that Barry ever really used. The phone rang only a couple of times before Barry's mother picked up.

It had taken almost a lifetime for Barry and his mother to see eye to eye. To rebuild the relationship that she'd so casually destroyed with homophobia during his formative years. Even on that day, the conversation on her end remained tentative. Barry spoke calmly and clearly like he was reading off a script. Because he was.

He told her that he was moving to Queensland. That he'd had enough of Adelaide, and that he wanted nothing more to do with her. He had not forgiven her. He never would. This was to be their last conversation. She told him that she loved him, and Robert took the phone from the older man's face and hung up.

'Good boy.' John grinned down at him. 'Shame you're a fucking paedo.'

He turned on the tape player and clamped the pliers onto the first of Barry's toes and squeezed. The other two held Barry down and gagged him. One by one, all ten toes were crushed to a pulp. The nails dislodged to patter in the bathtub. Next, John fetched out the little cudgels and the new machine that they'd purchased to administer electric shocks, and Robert was given his chance to finally get his own back for the years of molestation that he'd suffered at the hands of Barry Lane. The abuse he'd believed was love.

There was very little left intact of Barry by the time that he was finished, and Robert was exhausted to the point that he could barely stand. It fell to John and Thomas to wrap the broken-up body in plastic and transfer it into the back of Barry's car. John whistled as he got into the car. It was considerably nicer than his own. 'Reckon I'm keeping this one.'

He did not bring Thomas Trevilyan with him to Snowtown. He did not trust the man that far, not yet. That sort of trust had to be earned over time. One betrayal was not sufficient to win John over. He needed more. Instead, he dropped the young man off at his old apartment and helped him settle back in before they parted ways.

Back at the bank vault, it was simple enough to load Barry's remains into the same barrel of acid that Michael had been stuffed into, though it did result in one of the teenage boy's legs poking up above the surface. John looked down into the tangled mess of filthy old man and young teenage limbs and couldn't help but think that in death, he'd given Barry just what he'd always wanted. With a hand saw, he removed Michael's foot at the ankle and pushed it down into the acid alongside the rest before putting the lid back on the barrel.

It had been a good day's work, and in addition to dealing with the living loose end himself, they'd secured Barry's house so that they were free to come and go as often as was necessary to find the materials that they needed. They wouldn't even need to run the risk of changing anything with social services, just grab Barry's ID and bank his considerable benefit cheques for cash.

John had no concerns about running out of targets for their campaign. There were enough names pasted up on his wall to last a lifetime, and that was before anyone else crossed him, or crossed his path.

Unfortunately for John, it seemed that luck still was not on his side. Even as he started gearing up for the next target on his list, new dangers to the whole enterprise presented themselves.

After the error with the cheques, more interest was being taken in Suzanne Allen's case, and payments were going to be halted if she did not call the offices and confirm that nothing was untoward – a requirement that was going to necessitate something frankly miraculous on John's part, given the length of time the woman had been dead and buried.

Making matters worse, Thomas Trevilyan, their little double agent, was breaking under the pressure. Entrusting the secret of a murder and ongoing fraud to a man plagued his whole life by mental illness had been a serious miscalculation on John's part, something that the rest of the gang were quick to point out – behind his back.

Once more, John required a convincing actor to play one of his victims, and this time he turned to the mother of the last failure. Jodie Elliot, the sister of Mark's hated wife, a woman of such limited intelligence that he'd often compared her unfavourably to his mentally disabled victims when talking about her with friends. The appeal of using her was both that her simplicity made her easy to manipulate and that the deeper that he could involve her whole family in his criminal enterprises, the more incapable Elizabeth would be of ever turning her knowledge of his activities against him.

Yet even as simple as she was, he did not have the level of control over Jodie that he required to force her into impersonating a dead woman for him. She and her son had now moved in with Mark and his wife, limiting the amount of time John could feasibly spend with the woman without risk of his behaviour being discovered. With limited time to solidify their relationship and resolve his problems, he was forced to do something he found distasteful. He began sleeping with Jodie. Even as much as he viewed her as subhuman, he still did it because it got him what he needed. After the act was done, he felt sick to his stomach. All of his childhood trauma came rushing back to him.

It didn't matter that he was the strong one now, pinning someone else down. All that mattered was that he'd been forced to have sex against his will. Forced by circumstances this time, rather than by the powerful hands of his tormentors, but still forced. What made matters worse was the simple fact that he was going to be handing Jodie control of the situation, even if she was too stupid to realise it. He was putting himself in her power by having her impersonate Suzanne. Giving her the sort of material that could put him behind bars. All of which meant that this couldn't just be a one-time thing. He had to keep stringing Jodie along forever, or at least until he could get some other kind of emotional hold over her.

She made the call and, somehow, despite her meandering off-script and chatting away with the person on the other end of the line, she managed to get the situation resolved. John breathed a sigh of relief.

Still shaken from what that had taken out of him, John decided not to overexpose himself to the rest of the gang while manipulating their wayward companion, taking only Robert, his most trustworthy accomplice, with him when he went to confront Thomas about his breakdown.

John understood what Barry never could have. Despite the man's bulk, Thomas was weak. Mentally, he was weak. If he was crumbling after just a few months of guilt, then it would take only a little push to put an end to him once and for all.

John had expected the application of a little pressure to be all it would take to send the man into another manic-depressive spiral, resulting in his suicide or at least his commitment to a mental asylum, where nobody would believe a word that he said.

What they found in Trevilyan's run-down flat was not the gibbering lunatic that they'd been expecting or hoping for. Thomas appeared numb and confused, speaking only in monotone. Like the pressure had burnt his brain out entirely. He was a soldier in his own mind, and now that he'd seen some action and realised that he didn't have the stomach for it, he had no idea what to do with the rest of his life. Everything he was had been tied up in this idea of himself as a soldier. Without it, he felt lost. The death, the torture, they'd pushed him past his limits. When John tried to talk to him, he found the man to be almost catatonic. A living, ticking time bomb.

Despite it all, Thomas still followed orders when they were barked at him. When John ordered him out and into the car, he went without question. Mark had plenty of questions for John about what exactly he had planned, but John, feeling discretion was the better part of valour, kept his answers to himself until they were out of Trevilyan's earshot.

It was a long drive out to the Adelaide Hills, but through it all Thomas said nothing, did nothing, just passively observed and obeyed as he thought he was meant to. To John, sitting beside him in the driver's seat of Barry's old car, it felt like the times he'd driven a car with a dog beside him staring out at the scenery with no idea of what was coming next.

They headed out deeper into the wilds along dirt roads as far as they'd take them before climbing out and heading further still into the woods, off the beaten tracks, until they were far from anywhere a casual hiker might come along. It was here that Robert pulled out the noose he'd been tying behind Thomas in the car. Finding as sturdy a branch as they could, the murderers looped the rope up and over before tying it around the tree's trunk. John put down the old wooden box that he'd been carrying along with him and ordered Thomas up onto it.

The big man shook his head, tears and snot streaming down his face. It seemed as though John took pity on him for a moment, because he stopped barking commands and took a hold on the man's shoulders. Telling him it was alright. That everything was going to be alright. That sometimes a general had to sacrifice his soldiers for the greater good. For the mission. He told him that he'd played his part well. That he'd been a good soldier. That he was proud of the man who was now little more than a blubbering wreck.

When John stepped back and barked his order to mount the box this time. Thomas stepped up. The box wobbled beneath his feet as he shook and sobbed, but a calming hand on his back from John was all that it took to still him while Mark secured the rope around Thomas's throat, pulling it tight.

Both of the killers stepped back then and saluted Thomas. He saluted them back, and it was suddenly too much for John. He burst out laughing.

The last thing that Thomas felt was the sharp sting of betrayal as he realised that they'd just been stringing him along the whole time. He wasn't part of their mission. He was a joke to them. His anger rose and he was ready to roar at his killers, but that was the moment that John kicked the box away.

Despite the precautions that they had taken to isolate the site of their killing, the body was discovered within a month, but given Thomas Trevilyan's laundry list of mental issues, it was ruled a suicide almost immediately. John kept a newspaper clipping of the report on it instead of his usual, more visceral, trophies.

The War at Home

Throughout all of this, life had not magically ground to a halt. John may have been constantly juggling all of the commitments that he'd made to keep his conspiracy in operation, but that did not mean that the people whose lives he'd touched simply stopped when he was not around. Each and every one of them was trying to deal with their own troubles in whatever way worked. For Jamie Vlassakis, heroin was what worked.

John had always made his opinion on drugs abundantly clear. Drug addicts were subhuman, the same as disabled people, but worse, because they'd chosen to be like that instead of nature deciding for them.

The idea of Jamie becoming an addict and losing complete control of his life wasn't just an emotional blow to John, of course. The boy had information that could destroy John. He may not have been physically involved in any of the murders following the death of Ray Davies, but he was very aware of all John's criminal enterprises, the fraud, the murders, even Snowtown. He knew about it all because John had trusted him completely. Treated him like a son.

But Jamie was not his son. He did not have a father's authority over the boy, and it was becoming increasingly apparent that the hold he did have over the boy was considerably more tenuous than he'd originally believed. Jamie had friends of his own, a life of his own, beyond John's reach. And that life began to intrude on the little pocket universe that John had carved out for himself in the most uncomfortable of ways.

Gavin Porter was sitting on his sofa one day when he came home from handling his business, stoned out of his mind and grinning up at John. They were about the same age, but they had clearly lived two very different lives. Gavin was practically skeletal, haggard from years of substance abuse and hard living, while John had the musculature of a man who did heavy manual labour. Not the showy bodybuilder's muscles that got strutted down the beach, muscles built for their power, not their look.

He'd have thrown the junkie out that very moment if Jamie hadn't come back into the room with the same glazed expression on his face as Gavin and made some introductions. Porter was a friend from Victoria who needed somewhere to stay for a little while until he got settled in the new city. There was an unspoken challenge in Jamie's words. Daring John to object. Instead, John did what he did best – he switched out his violent rage for smooth charm. 'You should have said something, I'd have made up the sofa bed for him! Here, let me get you boys a beer. Did you need something to eat?'

He laid it on thick, but by the end of the day, he had both Jamie and Gavin convinced that he wasn't going to let the junkie on his sofa be a bone of contention between him and his adoptive son. He would not demand that the boy choose between him and heroin. That was not a battle of hearts and minds that anyone could win.

John just had to tolerate it. Grit his teeth and get through it. Like so many other parts of his life that had become unpalatable of late. His visits to Jodie. The onerous task of all the legwork collecting cheques and cashing them with the right IDs on hand.

Things that once would have made him feel powerful and victorious now left him tired. And every time he came home to the place that was meant to be his sanctuary, there was this useless junkie, this waste of space, taking up his space. Sitting in his seat. Eating his food. Sleeping under his roof. It grated on John, but still not enough to risk disrupting the tenuous relationship he was clinging to with Jamie.

That changed in an instant when he came home exhausted one day, slumped down onto the sofa, and felt a sharp stabbing in his side. A hypodermic needle. Used and discarded. It wasn't enough that the drugs and all their paraphernalia were in his house, now it was in him. All the filthy diseases that the junkie had were in him.

This was the final straw that broke his iron will. His commitment to easing back into Jamie's good graces and pushing the junkie out, much the same way he had wedged himself between Robert and Barry, was instantly and irrevocably obliterated in the face of this latest insult.

Gavin Porter was out in the driveway working on his car. In reality, that mostly meant lying under it and tinkering for a while, then falling asleep in the passenger seat when the heroin really knocked him out. All it took was a phone call and Robert hopped in his truck, loaded up an empty barrel and then rolled around.

By the time that he arrived, the sun was down and John was already waiting in the driveway to guide him into place. Rage written in every line on his face. The rage never really left John, not really. It was always there, just under the surface mask of whatever emotions he was acting out. That was why lying and manipulating people came so easily to him. He wasn't faking his response to the one thing; he was faking his response to everything. It all blended together into one long masquerade. Robert felt singularly blessed to be the one who got to see John with the mask off.

The mask came off when John opened the back door of Gavin's car, climbed in behind his sleeping body and reached around the headrest with a tyre-iron to pin it to the sleeping addict's throat. He pulled with all his strength, feet up on the back of the seat, his face flushing red, coming truly alive, as he let his rage out. It wasn't enough to choke the man. It wasn't enough to crush his windpipe or cut off the blood supply to his brain. John was pulling on that metal tool hard enough that Robert feared it would snap. Like he was trying to pull it right through Gavin's neck and out the other side.

In the end, he did not decapitate the sleeping man, but he did enough damage that his neck was no longer recognizable as such. Robert rolled up the barrel, and John dropped the tyre iron in. Then, working together, they moved the limp corpse, dumping it in headfirst and then pushing and stamping on it until the lid fit back on top.

It took the two of them to lift the barrel back up into Robert's truck, and it took the two of them to unload it again at Snowtown bank because John had unleashed such force that he'd pulled every muscle in his arms and across his back in his fury. He had to direct Robert on the mix of chemicals to pour over the top of the corpse to make up his special mix to destroy all evidence.

He was almost asleep by the time that Robert dropped him back at home in the early hours of the morning, aching, satisfied, and desperate for his bed.

Jamie was sitting up waiting for him. He'd come home to find both John and Gavin missing, Gavin's car still sitting unlocked in the driveway, ensuring that he couldn't have gone far. He knew that something was wrong. He knew that John had done something. There was no accusation, just some very precise questions about where he'd been. Where Gavin was. What he'd been doing all day. John stonewalled his way through most of the conversation before finally informing Jamie that they would talk about it in the morning.

Come morning, Jamie was nowhere to be seen, having slunk out to stay with some of his other junkie friends. Gavin's car was gone by the time that he got back a few days later. All trace of his belongings, too. He knew exactly what had happened without John having to explain. He explained, very carefully, that he'd been upset over the death of a friend, not that he was upset with John. In turn, John gave him a lecture on his personal philosophy about drugs. They were an escape for the weak, for people who didn't have the courage to face reality head-on and exert their will over it. John wanted to help Jamie, but the first step to walking for himself was to let go of the crutches he'd been using.

If nothing else, John was a convincing orator, and despite the recent distance between them, Jamie was still desperate for the older man's approval, just as he'd been conditioned to be. He was literally willing to forgive murder so long as John made the insult and injury against him right.

Luckily, John knew just how to do that. Every day for years now, John had sat down beside Jamie and just listened to whatever he wanted to say. Sometimes they'd talk about nothing at all, sometimes it became an impromptu therapy session when John willingly admitted fragments of his past in exchange for teasing new knowledge of Jamie's past out of him. It would only be little hints and traces of the truth. Neither one of them could afford to face what had been done to them head-on. Not if they wanted to cling to their bravado and sanity. But from the hints and scraps, John had pieced together Jamie's sad story all too easily. Not just the fact that his old man had sexually abused him, but that he'd invited in Jamie's older stepbrother, Troy Youde, to do the same. It had become a game for the older boy to amuse himself with – molesting his little stepbrother. But for Jamie, it had been a humiliation too far. When an adult abused him, he could at least excuse himself as powerless against them, but when Troy did it, he had to admit his weakness. Troy was just another child, a bigger one, but still just a child. There was no way for Jamie to convince himself that he could not have resisted. It made him feel complicit in his abuse. It made him feel weak, pathetic, the victim.

John knew all of this even before Troy made his petition to come and live with Elizabeth, desperate to escape from the oppressive shadow of the man who had abused him once Jamie had escaped his reach. Elizabeth was all heart when confronted with another victim of her ex-husband's violence, but ultimately the decision fell to John, who made careful eye contact with Jamie before giving permission.

It felt like the ultimate betrayal to Jamie, and he was up from the kitchen table and storming out the door before John intercepted him, wrapping him in a fierce hug, pinning him in place and whispering in his ear. 'This is your chance. This is your chance to get him back. Don't walk out on me. Don't walk out on this chance.'

It took a moment for the words to penetrate Jamie's rage, and even then, they didn't really sink in. He struggled to escape from the older man's grasp, wrestling to break out, to get out, to run. Then all of a sudden, he froze as he realised exactly what John was offering him. Before, when they'd killed, it had been impersonal. Part of the mission. A chance to exorcise their demons on some unwilling body. But this wasn't that; this was revenge pure and simple. A chance to finally pay Troy back for what he'd done.

Troy moved in and John greeted him with open arms. He got him all set up with a room of his own and told him that they'd unpack the rest of his stuff in the morning. It would never be unpacked. The few essentials that Troy took out of his cases were packaged back up the following morning before being taken off to the dump. Everything except for his ID and benefits paperwork.

Troy woke up in the middle of the night to find John, Jamie, Robert and Mark looming over him in the shadows. The Live album 'Throwing Copper' was playing, just as it had played in the comfort of the killing room at the Snowtown Bank.

For the first time, Jamie took the lead, but just a moment later, Mark and Robert lunged in to help secure Troy and give the younger man all the time in the world to take him apart. First, his fists rained down on his stepbrother. Then out came the bludgeons. The tools of torture. Troy's screams were muffled with a pillow after he'd been dragged from his bed onto the empty patch of floor that they'd carefully left clear for this very purpose. For hours, they let Jamie work through his frustrations and turn his trauma into someone else's pain, but in the end, Troy's flesh gave out before Jamie's rage. Even with him dead, the vengeance wasn't enough, so John put Jamie's residual fury to work dismembering Troy so that it was a simple matter to toss the parts into the barrel that Mark had rolled in for that very purpose. It went to Snowtown with all the rest, and Jamie went right back to being John's lapdog.

He didn't quit heroin by any stretch, but at least some small part of the pressure that had been driving him to douse himself in drugs every day had been eased. His step-father remained out of reach for now, but he felt certain that someday John would find a way. His faith in the man and the mission was renewed, and his reignited passion seemed to bring that spark back for the rest of them, too. Everyone was raring to get back to the great work with all the threats to their security eliminated. Everyone except Mark, whose wife had been asking entirely too many questions about where all the money passing through their bank account was coming from, where it was going, and what exactly John Bunting's involvement in their personal finances was.

Mark brought the problem to John, who was of the personal opinion that a little bit of wife-murder might be in order, but instead settled for a back-up option that would also eliminate one of the other loose ends that they'd left in their wake while they clumsily tried to get the operation running properly. Mark didn't want his wife dead, but he could not give a damn about

Jodie or her disabled son. The sudden disappearance of either one would be sufficient to shock Elizabeth Haydon into complicit silence, but given that John still found he had ongoing use for Jodie, both in a carnal and practical sense, that left them with only Fred Brooks.

Fred had unwittingly become a source of information for his aunt regarding what exactly John had been using him for. His simple and straightforward nature entirely unsuited to this sort of skulduggery, he had assumed that as the wife of one of the conspirators, Elizabeth was entirely aware of her husband's actions and schemes and spilt all the beans the moment that she started talking openly about them.

John and Robert killed him in Mark's own home, dragging the boy out of his bed and brutalising him only briefly before choking the life out of him. It was a matter of practicality more than of pleasure despite both of the men involved wishing it were more. Mark then swept in and assisted John in carrying the boy's body out to his car. Fred weighed almost nothing, and either one of them could have borne him without difficulty, but carrying together was the plan that they had laid out ahead of time, so that was what they did.

In Snowtown, Fred was deposited neatly into one of the empty barrels and the acid formula poured over him. Retrieval of his personal goods from the house was almost entirely unnecessary since Mark already lived there and had full control over the boy's finances. The payments that Fred used to receive to subsidise living with his disabilities had been under the control of the cabal since the day that he arrived. The only difference was that now Mark no longer had to dole it out to him as an allowance.

The death of Fred marked a sudden change in the attitudes of both Elizabeth Haydon and Jodie, with the former suddenly developing a healthy respect for John, a least to his face, and the latter cutting off their relationship entirely. She would no longer be viable for calls made impersonating the deceased Suzanne

Allen, but neither would she be talking to anyone else. She was too scared of John to even touch him now, ironically making her attractive to him for the first time in their entire relationship.

He relished being in her presence, feeling the dread radiating off her, but he never forced sexual contact even though there would have been no way for her to resist him. He held himself to higher standards than that. He'd never be like the paedophile rapists who'd had their way with him. He was better than that. He was a soldier in the war against all that. Even now, after so many bodies, so many people who had nothing to do with his little crusade, he still clung to that justification for dear life.

Reaping the Rewards

Gary O'Dwyer lived alone on Frances Street. He had no social life to speak of, no friends, no family. He subsisted on benefits payments from the government after a tragic car accident in his twenties resulted in his being permanently intellectually disabled. He could still remember what his life was like before the accident. He could still remember living like everyone else in Adelaide, but he couldn't do it now. Even if it was so close that he could taste it, normality remained forever outside his reach, blocked off by a fog of confusion.

When Jamie began to visit with him, Gary could not pierce that fog of confusion to work out why. The other young man seemed nice enough, friendly enough. He seemed to enjoy Gary's company, whether Gary was capable of stringing together a coherent thought that day or not. As for Gary, these visits rapidly became the highlight of his life. He was always there waiting, with nothing else to fill up his days or his mind but the banalities that Jamie filled his living room with. When more pointed questions snuck into the conversation, he was not even aware of it. Day by day, week by week, Jamie came into his home, chatted with him like they were friends, and gathered all of the information that John asked him to. Then, just as abruptly as he'd started showing up, Jamie stopped.

It was only a few days later that his new houseguest arrived, letting themselves in through the back door that they knew was left unlocked, because Jamie had noted it. Walking through the house like they knew the floorplan, because Jamie had drawn it out for them. Not even bothering with the empty bedroom, because they knew that Gary fell asleep in front of the television every night.

The first time that Gary realised something was wrong was when the television went silent and a tape turned on, playing Live's album 'Throwing Copper', John's favourite soundtrack to commit torture to.

There was never any suggestion that Gary was a paedophile. Just that he was an easy target. John couldn't even reach to his usual neo-Nazi justifications of removing inferior genetics from the breeding population since Gary's disability was a result of an accident. He had committed no 'crime' even in John's twisted worldview. There was no reason for him to die other than the fact that it was convenient for John to get his money.

The routine of torture and murder had been improved upon from victim to victim. The beatings were lighter now, with John believing that they did too much to disable the victim's ability to understand what was happening to them, but the other torture had become much more elaborate. A Variac was attached to Gary's body in various places, and an electrical current was run through it until the skin around the contact pads had blackened to a crisp. Then they were moved and the whole thing started over again. Electricity had become John's new favourite toy, and he delighted in sharing it with the others, taking turns to see who could draw the most wretched screams out of their victim. In the isolation of his home, they drew out his death for as long as possible. This was entertainment for them, this was sport, stripped of all the moralisation and lies. Gary was weak, and they were bored. Schoolyard bullies taken to the ultimate extreme.

When everyone who wanted a turn was done and the album had finished up its runtime, Gary was dead. They loaded his corpse in a barrel, drove it out to Snowtown, filled it up with the chemical soup, and went on about their days with a new income stream flowing.

The money was piling up now, every one of the cabal drawing a healthy wage from their enterprise and living at a level of financial security that they'd never experienced before in their lives. Repeatedly, they had been shown that John was willing to kill to keep his secrets, but even without that fear, there were more than enough reasons to just leave things alone. Even Jodie was by and large taken care of, thanks to the money Mark received, so that the loss of her stepson and her fear for her own life were balanced with the comforts that she was rewarded for her silent compliance.

In the entire social network that John had established around Adelaide, there was only one person who had both enough information about his activities and a willingness to use it against him. Elizabeth Haydon.

Despite all evidence to the contrary, Elizabeth had continued to work on her husband throughout all of this time in the belief that she could win him over from John. Her outright criticism of John had come to a halt, but her questioning never did. She badgered her husband constantly, wheedling out more and more information about the fraud, gathering names, dates, and locations, and digging through their family's personal finances to discover exactly where everything was coming from and going to.

A professional forensic accountant could not have done as solid a job as Elizabeth, and as Mark's wife, she had full access to all the information that the bank held about him. By the end, she probably had a better grasp on everything that was happening with John's money than John himself. Every date and time of a deposit was marked, every payment that went out filed away.

She could prove the fraud easily at this point, but there were other loose ends that she meant to tie off before she went to the police. There was no question in her mind that John would identify her as the culprit if somebody turned on the cabal, and she needed to be sure that whatever evidence she provided to the police would be insurmountable. She had to bury John before he could bury her.

She suspected the murders, but without any physical evidence, she could not prove them. There was plenty of hearsay and convenient timing, but nothing solid enough to put John behind bars for the duration of the trial. He could walk away from fraud. She needed those murders to put him down for good.

As comfortable as her current living situation was, it was a gilded cage, and Elizabeth Haydon had no intention of remaining within it. If she could save Mark, trading her testimony for him to avoid jail time, then that was what she meant to do, but she refused to live her whole life in fear of a man like John Bunting.

She was convinced that her sister could be convinced to testify against John if she thought that her safety from his vengeance could be guaranteed, but that just added to the pressure. If Elizabeth made a mistake and pulled the trigger too soon, then it wouldn't just be her that took the brunt of John's fury. Jodie would, too. Probably worse than Elizabeth would, if truth be told. They'd have to kill Elizabeth, but Jodie could be kept in this living hell forever. Too scared to run in case she was chased.

The cabal had been careful to cover their tracks in case of police interest or investigations by the government into where all their disability benefit cheques were disappearing to, but they had never thought to build in any protections against each other. Elizabeth had the same access as one of the founding members of their little murder club, so she was able to delve far deeper into their affairs than anyone from the outside ever could.

Mark was aware that she was up to something throughout this period, but it is unlikely even he knew the extent of her research. He kept John updated on the questions that she had been asking. John in turn kept a balance in his head of the risk versus the reward of allowing Elizabeth to go on breathing.

In November of 1998, that balance tipped against her. The latest round of questions that she had been asking related to the rental of the property in Snowtown, entirely in Mark's name, but using John's money. She'd made passing comments to Mark that she'd like to visit up there sometime. She was too close. Much too close to making the trip herself. From the exterior, nothing was incriminating about the bank, but if she availed herself of Mark's key, then such a trip would have very different results.

Mark and Jodie were out for the day, John painstakingly aware of their movements as he was all of the pieces in the game that he was playing. He and Robert slipped into the house and surprised Elizabeth in the living room. It had never even occurred to her that they might come for her in broad daylight. Even knowing how cocky John was, for some reason, she just hadn't been able to picture it.

John's face was split into a broad grin from the moment that he laid eyes on her. He had been waiting for this day for a very long time. And the smile only got wider when she yelped out, 'Mark won't let you.'

John laughed. 'Mark's the one who told us to do it.'

It may not have been true, but it certainly had the desired effect, dropping Elizabeth into a pit of despair that she would not climb out of until the end. All of the fight went out of her with that final betrayal, and as the men rushed in at her, she broke down in sobs.

Out of respect for Mark, they did not commit the usual levels of mutilation and torture on this latest victim. There was also the fact that she was a woman. All their previous victims had been men. Just like the ones that had abused them in their own tragic pasts. Neither one of them had been tormented by a woman, so the rage was only as deep as John's dislike for her. It had been a long time building, but it still wasn't anywhere near as foundational to his personality as the rage he felt towards other men.

In the span of a few minutes, Elizabeth was borne down to the ground, pinned in place and quietly strangled to death. It was the second murder that they had committed in this house, and once more it left them feeling hollow.

They had not been allowed their usual pleasure in the slaughter. It was killing for the sake of seeing the victim dead, not for the sake of the killing itself. It felt vaguely sacrilegious. Like they had not gone through the correct rituals.

That same sense of wrongness clung to them as time went on. Mark came home once the deed was done, as he had been told to, but at the sight of his dead wife, he began to weep.

The jovial camaraderie that usually carried them on past the moment of killing just wasn't there that day, and that being the case, the task of dumping the body into a barrel and loading it into the back of Mark's pickup was just joyless manual labour. They drove to Snowtown in silence, the only break from the rumble of the road beneath them were Mark's sniffling sobs. Whatever her faults, he had loved Elizabeth. He had wanted to avoid this, he'd been trying, desperately, to avoid it. Why couldn't she have just left well enough alone?

With her body deposited in the vault, John did what he could to cheer his old friend Mark up. Now that Elizabeth was gone, he'd be free to do whatever he wanted again, whenever he wanted. He wouldn't need to keep his spending hidden or pretend that he wasn't chasing after some other girl. He'd be able to live like a free man again.

This pep talk only seemed to make Mark even more miserable, which in turn began to concern John. He hadn't predicted that Mark might become this close with the woman that he'd married. It didn't make sense to him or fit into his worldview. Women existed for sex, maybe a little bit of a cuddle if you were feeling soft, but love had always eluded him, and he'd come to the conclusion that it didn't actually exist. It was just another one of those lies that polite society used to justify its bad habits.

Except none of that was enough to explain Mark's ongoing breakdown. As the next year rolled around, he went on growing more and more distant. Spending less time drinking with his mates and more time alone, lost in his own thoughts. Jodie was still around, of course, but she was a zombie by this point, moving soundlessly through the house, talking to nobody and doing nothing with herself. Her son and her sister both gone, and death waiting for her the moment that she stepped out of line.

The police had been around, asking them both questions, after Elizabeth went missing. John hadn't taken all the details into account when he made his decision. He'd been so eager to rid himself of that thorn in his side that the usual due diligence to ensure that his victims had no friends or family that would miss them had been skipped. Elizabeth had a brother. Garion Sinclair had been expecting to meet his sister the day after she was killed and immediately reported her as a missing person to the police after Mark and Jodie had failed to justify her absence. It took some legwork to get the ball rolling with the police, but Garion was nothing if not determined. He continued making his reports of Elizabeth being missing until officers were dispatched to investigate, and once a case had been opened, there was no going back. Inch by inch, it began to move forward.

Mark had discovered the collected research against John and the rest of the cabal in Elizabeth's belongings as he cleared out the house of any reminder of her. He destroyed all of the evidence that she had bundled together in a fire, along with as much of the paperwork that she'd used to collect the information as possible. He didn't tell the others about this so as not to hear his beloved wife's name dragged through the dirt again. John didn't need his mind set at ease over the murder. There was no sting of conscience holding him back, and if anything, justification would have just made him more willing to kill again.

John wasn't worried about the police. Not yet. Mark knew how to handle himself under questioning, and Jodie was still his creature. But he did still struggle to understand Mark's degenerating mental state.

Fair enough. He wasn't getting sex on the regular anymore, but all this depression seemed a bit excessive. Trailing off in the middle of conversations. Moping around the house all the time. Crying in front of other men. It was a sign of weakness. Mental weakness. John couldn't have him cracking up. He couldn't replace Mark. The idea of even trying was enough to send him into a panic. He needed to win Mark back over as fast as possible. He had to bond the man to the pack again so that he'd never consider turning on them.

Taste of Victory

To John's mind, there was no better bonding experience than communal murder, so by spring of 1999, when it became clear that Mark wasn't going to pull back from the brink of the abyss on his own, John set to finding them a victim.

His list of potential victims was not any shorter in 1999 than it had been back when he first started out. For every person that he had personally eliminated, a half dozen had moved away to escape the escalating harassment that they received at his hands. Yet somehow, he was constantly finding new people whom he firmly believed were deserving of death. As the place where all the outcasts of society were dumped, Salisbury North had a burgeoning gay population, along with an equally large number of ex-convicts attempting to make a new life for themselves. At the intersection of these two communities, John found his favoured prey, vulnerable now that they were released to the threats of incarceration if they stepped out of line or if certain rumours about them were shouted loud enough that it seemed they were a threat to others.

Yet when the time came to find his next victim, John looked closer to home. He'd become entirely too accustomed to the ease of killing those closest to him and his little family of killers. He did not have to spend weeks on reconnaissance or research into their finances. Everything was readily available.

Jamie had served him well during the process with Gary, and he had been receiving a cut of that man's disability stipend in payment for services rendered now that John was relatively confident that he wouldn't shoot any money he received directly into his arm.

Jamie had never been as enthusiastic about killing as John, not since that first time. He did it when he had to or when he had a personal stake, but it was never a pleasure for him the way it was for the rest of them. He got catharsis from unleashing his rage, but none of the fierce joy. That's why John had found him other things to do – to keep him in the loop but held back from anything that might upset him.

While Jamie had nothing but affection for John, his relationship with his mother was a little strained, and his father had been the abuser who haunted his nightmares. Yet still, he couldn't extricate himself entirely from that side of his family. His father had other sons, the children of his new partners that he treated as his own, sons who seemed to have suffered none of the same abuse that Jamie had, confusing him even more about why his father had chosen him and him alone to be the victim of all his perverse lusts.

It left him in an awkward, halfway position with his step-siblings. In one way drawn to them and the promise of a normal familial relationship, but equally repulsed by the knowledge of where they came from. It didn't help matters that they seemed to be living a perfectly normal life while he was pushed to the fringes of society, slipping through the cracks into the grasp of John Bunting and his ilk.

It was that very ambivalence that John preyed on when he asked Jamie to reach out to his step-brother David. It had already been established that David's father was the kind of person reluctant to have anything to do with the police, and his mother no longer seemed to be a feature in his life, at least according to the intelligence that had been filtering back to John through Jamie. David Johnson had left behind the dysfunction of his childhood and was on course to a brighter future. With a good education and plans to do great things with himself, he nonetheless stayed in touch with his step-brother, since Jamie had always been kind to him, more or less out of spite toward their father's attempts to pit them against each other.

They didn't see each other regularly, but they would both go out of their way to keep in touch. To call on the other's birthday and keep up with each other's lives – even if Jamie's life didn't tend to have as many highlights as David could share.

It wasn't hard for John to start twisting David's words around. To make his meetings with Jamie into a mockery of a healthy familial relationship with just a tilt of his head and a smirk. All the kind words became sarcastic jibes in Jamie's mind. All the praise, contempt. He had no foundations to build a healthy and happy relationship of any sort, whether it was familial or just a friendship, and John preyed on his insecurity as surely as he had preyed on any of the people now loaded into barrels over in a vault under Snowtown.

John began to refer to David exclusively as 'the faggot'. He made a point of differentiating the soft life that David got to live from the hard life that Jamie had suffered through in every single conversation. David was on track for greater things. He was going to be somebody. Make something of his life. Everything that Jamie never could. He made it seem like David was doing it all just to rub Jamie's nose in how much better he was than his pathetic, junkie, criminal step-brother.

By the time that John was finally ready to reel David in as a victim, Jamie was almost angry enough to kill the man himself. More than willing to throw him to the wolves.

David was in the market for a computer, so Jamie fabricated a story about knowing someone who had one for sale at well under the market price. Knowing about Jamie's moderately criminal background, David might think that he was getting stolen goods, but he would feel safe in making the purchase because his big brother was along for the ride.

They drove out to Snowtown together, Jamie in the driver's seat, chatting and smiling all the way, just like he always had. It put David at ease, just the way that it always did. Jamie didn't even have to pretend, not really. All he had to do was stop himself thinking about what came next. So long as he didn't think about what he was going to do next, what was going to be done to David next, then he could go on rolling along as if he were helping out his brother, his friend. It was easy. After a lifetime of having to partition off parts of himself as too unacceptable for public consumption, after having to keep John's secrets and watching from the sidelines as his adoptive father shifted and snapped from one persona to the next, manipulating and lying and becoming someone new for every new person that he met, after all of that, pretending that everything was going to be alright – the same lie that he'd been telling himself since he was old enough to remember – was so easy it barely even felt like a lie at all.

When they arrived at the bank, Jamie walked David in ahead of him and locked the door, following along behind his step-brother to make sure he had no avenue of escape until he was in the office and that door could be locked behind him, too.

In the office, the whole gang set upon him, choking him out, attaching handcuffs to his wrists and threatening him with all sorts of horrific torture until he agreed to read out a script that they had prepared into a microphone that was hooked up to the computer that David thought he was there to buy. In the script, the fictional David that they had created for him to play announced that he was moving away from Adelaide. He made personalised declarations to everyone that John thought that he might be in contact with, severing all social ties.

He admitted to terrible, disgusting things that he could never have even conceived of doing. Told everyone that he was gay even though he'd never shown even the slightest inclination towards the same sex. Told everyone that he was a paedophile. All of the things that would have made him the perfect target for John's little cabal, captured in a recording that John could listen to whenever he wanted. To use whenever he wanted to throw any pursuit off track.

All of this time, John had been perfecting his methodology, finding new ways to protect himself and to extract the wealth of his targets.

David didn't have a welfare cheque for John to steal, but he did have something that none of the previous victims had: money in the bank. Jamie had assured John that David had a good chunk of money squirrelled away, just like everybody with a successful life. He had enough money to throw away on a home computer, after all. Something that even John, in all his sudden influx of cash, hadn't even thought of buying before now.

Unfortunately, when they went digging through David's wallet, the cash wasn't there. Just a bank card.

They hadn't moved on to the part of the day that John had been looking forward to the most. Not yet. And as it turns out, it was a good thing, too, because they needed to extract David's PIN to gain access to his money.

Like everything else, David was all set to give it up easily, certain that insurance would cover anything he lost after he went to the police, but then he was struck with a realisation. A realisation that had been slowly building throughout this whole ordeal. He had seen all of their faces. He knew John from the times that he'd dropped Jamie off at one of their meetups. He vaguely recognised others from his visits to Jamie's home. None of them seemed desperate or panicked. If he gave them his PIN, then they no longer needed him for anything. Previously, he'd assumed that meant that they'd just let him go when they didn't need anything else, but as he'd recited all of the things in the script, he began to get a sinking feeling in the pit of his stomach, like he'd swallowed a lead weight. If they didn't need him anymore, was he going to be allowed to walk out of the bank alive?

In an instant, he conceived of a plan – swapping out one of the numbers in his PIN with another. When they went to the bank and tried to use the card, it would fail. If they tried repeatedly, the teller might notice that they were using his card and call the police. It was a slim hope of intervention, but it was something. Something that might save him from what was now looking more and more like inevitable death.

John was suspicious, of course. Just as he'd been suspicious of everything that David had done up until this point. It was all too easy. They'd barely even had to hurt him before he started doing everything that they wanted. John knew that people outside of his usual social circles weren't as hardened to danger and strife, but it still struck him as far too easy. Like David hadn't really broken.

With the wrong PIN scribbled down on a piece of paper, John announced that they were going to go and test it before moving on to the next stage of the plan. He was going to remain at the bank with Mark and keep an eye on their hostage while Robert took Jamie to the bank in Port Wakefield to see if the information that they'd been given was correct. It was the best scenario that David could hope for, but for some reason, he couldn't shake the feeling that he was still doomed.

Jamie had to be ushered out of the room, his eyes still locked on David. Emotions were flickering over his face so quickly that David couldn't even hope to decipher them all. Was he sorry for delivering his step-brother to these maniacs? Was he pleased with himself? Neither one of the young men could say for certain.

What was certain, however, was that David's sense of impending doom was ever more prescient than he could have known. He had suspected that they'd try the PIN, come back angry, and rough him up if this Hail Mary attempt to save himself failed. He had assumed that despite their current roles as his tormenters, kidnappers, and robbers, he was surrounded by sane men who operated off some sort of logic. He could not know that death was its own reward, the way that the cabal knew. Not that knowing would have saved him.

When the other two were gone, off on the long drive to the nearest cash machine, John turned to Mark and gave him a smile. Mark wasn't much for smiling by that point in his life, but he recognised something unexpected on John's face. He walked over to the radio on the desk and switched it over to the CD player. 'Throwing Copper' began to play, the slow, almost gentle guitar riff of the first song building up from the silence.

Mark looked from John's mugging expression to the boy in the chair. He'd never been the one to start on them before. He'd never been the one on the front lines, serving more in a hands-off capacity as the crimes continued to escalate, handling the money and the logistics more than the actual act of violence itself. Yet now John was offering this boy up to him like a gift.

John slunk out of the room and came back with all the tools of the trade. The machinery for electrocution. The bludgeons. The tools. Mark didn't even notice. He'd closed in on David where he sat handcuffed to the chair and had started working him over with his bare hands.

When he stopped to breathe, John would press something new into his hands. A pair of pliers. A metal pipe. A pair of electrodes.

David was not strangled like so many of their victims. He had his head back and a long warbling scream pouring from his lips, sweet music to John's ears.

Mark was lost in the frenzy of it. Moving to the songs as they played without ever truly hearing them. His hands all red. His vision all red. The smile on his face was not faked for John's benefit. The weight that had been crushing him since Elizabeth died was lifted. All the weight that he carried for John and the others, all faded away. He only stopped when the music stopped. His arms felt numb from exhaustion, and the man cuffed to the chair... he barely looked human anymore. He was still alive, still breathing and sobbing, but there was so much damage, Mark couldn't understand why.

The sobbing and crying just confirmed to John what he'd already suspected, this David was weak. Soft. Unworthy of life. The battle lines in John's war had been drawn and redrawn so many times by now that they were a blur by this point. Everyone he considered less than him was a degenerate subhuman unworthy of life. He lived the fantasy that in the shoes of his victims, he would fight back, would overpower his oppressors and take his bloody revenge, just as he'd fantasised about doing to the boys who'd had their way with him when he was just a child. Every time that they failed to fight back, or to take their punishment with the kind of stoic perfection that he imagined that he could, they marked themselves as deserving of all the torments he could inflict. Even as he hurt them, it proved that they deserved to suffer more.

John was practically glowing at the sight of the brutality before him, and as Mark staggered back to flop down into a seat and catch his breath, John stepped forward into his place. There was a moment's silence, then the hour-long album started again, the first chords thrumming out. John stood there for a moment, just listening, smelling the blood on the air, muscles bunching and coiling beneath his t-shirt as he stretched and readied himself.

David's breath bubbled as it came out, a sob with every gasp, a shudder with every nerve ending in his body aflame. When the singer's voice came from the speakers, John laid in on David.

The album ran out its length, and by the time that it was over, there were only two people left to hear it. Somewhere in the middle of the second playthrough, David's strength had run out. There was only so much punishment that a body could take, and he had taken it all.

Jamie and Robert arrived back to find their co-conspirators still standing over the dead body of David Johnson. Jamie looked appalled at what they had done to him, but it was Robert who truly lost his temper. Not because they'd lost the money from David's account by killing him before they had confirmed that the PIN worked, but because they had killed without him. He had missed out on all of the fun. He'd put in all the work, and he'd received none of the rewards, and he was livid. Mark, still completely high on endorphins, and Jamie, distant enough from the pleasure of killing that he had no idea what Robert's real complaint was, both stood back from the two founding fathers of their little murder club as they squared off against each other.

John was speckled with blood, wide-eyed and throbbing with barely contained aggression, but still, he looked to be the saner of the two men. Robert was beyond livid at this betrayal. This was all that he lived for, and John had taken it from him, hoarded all of the joy for himself. They shared everything, that had always been the deal, and now John did this to satisfy himself and himself only? Jamie and Mark, at John's none-too-subtle prompting, took a little walk and left the men to talk.

John was more than capable of telling the truth when the situation warranted it. So that was what he did now. He explained how badly Mark had needed this. How close the other man had been to breaking and leaving them all high and dry. He was genuinely apologetic to Robert, treating him for the first time like a true equal instead of an acolyte and vowing to make it up to him.

In tense, angry silence, they began to work on David's body, tearing it apart into its component parts so that it could be carted down to the waiting barrel in the vaults more easily. John's knife slipped off a slick nub of bone and danced out, cutting a neat steak slice of meat from David's thigh. He stared at it for a long moment, then turned to Robert with a wide smile on his face. 'Fun doesn't have to be over.'

When Mark and Jamie returned to the back rooms of the bank, the smell of frying meat greeted them. Mark couldn't understand where it had come from, but Jamie already knew before they came through to the kitchenette and saw John there with a frying pan and a broad smile on his face. Robert was settled at the staff room table, a paper plate with a well-done steak sitting half-eaten in front of him. That same broad, bloody toothed grin on his face, too.

'Alright, fellas. Who wants some?'

Jamie could not stomach it, couldn't even countenance it, and he begged off. Mark may have truly tasted blood for the first time that day, but he wasn't ready for this to be his second course. Both of them were horrified in their own ways. John settled himself beside Robert and tucked into his thick cut of meat. Never taking his eyes off the other two. Daring them to say a thing.

It had taken no convincing for Robert. The people that they killed were no better than animals. This was what you did with an animal when you'd slaughtered it. They'd joked often enough about throwing a paedo on the barbie. How was this any different? There was a different joy to be taken in cannibalism from the actual act of murder, but John and Robert both took their time and revelled in it, cracking open a beer to toast a successful day.

Mark had never understood before that the killing truly wasn't about the money. He'd assumed John would be enraged at their failure to secure David's money, but it was an afterthought to him. An acceptable loss.

At least Mark and Jamie were cut loose after they had watched Robert and John finishing their meals. The other two could do what they wanted with the body so long as Jamie didn't have to watch any more. In due time, the rest of David was conveyed to one of the barrels down in the vault. The chemical mixture poured over him. The vault and barrels sealed.

He would be the last person that John Bunting and his friends killed, though that was probably small comfort to him.

Reaping What Was Sown

Garion Sinclair's campaign to discover what had happened to his sister never stopped. He devoted all of his energies to it. Pushing the police harder and harder to discover what had happened to her. While the police were not enjoying his harassment, there could be no denying that something was not right about the situation. Mark Haydon and Jodie Elliot had failed to account for Elizabeth's absence in a satisfactory manner, both providing similar, but notably different, accounts of what had happened to her. Like they had been given a vague script and both had gone off it in different places.

It was a minor slip, but one that they found repeated again and again, with their stories diverging further and further from the statement that they'd received from Garion Sinclair. For his part, Garion began pushing for the police to look at the family's money. He knew that Mark didn't work, yet somehow they could afford a house in a nice area. The police began to believe that this was all just some personal vendetta against a man who didn't live up to his brother-in-law's exacting standards, but the incongruity of the statements was there, staring back at them. They had to follow the investigation through to its natural conclusion.

Their investigation found more and more inexplicable details as time went on until finally their suspicions had been raised enough that they began pursuing the Haydon family's financial records as Sinclair had demanded from the start, knowing at least a little of his sister's suspicions that something was awry.

The incongruities in those accounts were so massive that the one detective who'd been looking into Elizabeth's disappearance suddenly found that he needed more manpower to pursue all of the leads. Everywhere that they looked, there were more missing people, missing people who had a steady income flowing, indirectly, into Haydon's account.

It became clear to the police that something much bigger was afoot, but until they had a fuller idea of what that bigger picture might be, they had to keep their distance. With the amount of money readily available to Haydon, it would be a simple matter for him to take flight if they showed their hand too soon. His entanglement with John Bunting was a matter of financial record, as was his connection to each of the other members of the little cabal through the years. This covert investigation led to dead end after dead end, more missing people or dead people everywhere that they looked.

Almost all of the money flowing out of the accounts was delivered to members of the cabal through convoluted means, all of it except for the rent on a property in the distant and tiny town of Snowtown.

The police decided to take a risk and investigate the property, taking care to ensure that they had all of their paperwork in place and no direct contact with the landlord on the property until the very last moment. Their caution paid dividends in terms of evidence, but it had an unexpected cost. David Johnson died just a few short days before they finally gained access to the bank in Snowtown on the 20th of May.

Creeping into the dusty and mostly disused building in silence, the police spread out to search for evidence. Everywhere that the cabal had walked was clearly marked by footprints in the dust. They came upon the computer sitting on a desk in a now empty room and booted it up. They came upon the kitchenette with a frying pan and cutlery still resting in the drying rack. They followed the trail down into the dark depths of the building, to the doors of the vault where they hung open.

With the computer on, there were few files to browse, just some audio files that had been recorded recently. They played them, out of curiosity more than anything else. David Johnson's confession, unedited to remove the sounds of threats or violence. The officers did not know what to make of it. They were here looking into a missing wife, and somehow they'd uncovered a confession to far worse crimes, extracted with violence. Nothing about the situation made a lick of sense.

The officers down at the vaults pulled the door open enough to squeeze through into the pitch black, relying on their torchlight to guide them deeper. The barrels loomed up out of the empty void, the only things down here in the vault. Giving the closest one a knock and a shove, they established that the barrels were full, but full of what they couldn't say.

Grabbing a screwdriver from where John had left it in his toolbox, they pried the lid off the closest barrel, and the true horror of what they had walked into washed over them. The cool air, the chemicals, the sealed barrels, they had all done their work to contain the smell, but now that the seal had been broken, it washed out over the officers and the whole building. The stench of death and decay. Still, they maintained their composure for long enough to look down into the chemical soup and catch a glimpse of a dismembered body. Then they had to flee, desperately seeking out the toilets, failing, and settling for the janitor's sink as a ready receptacle for their nausea's natural conclusion.

Specialists were called in. The other barrels were opened. The big picture that the police had been looking for became abruptly and sickeningly clear.

The crime scene had to be sealed, but it was done with a level of cunning that most would have thought beyond the rural Australian police. Everything was left looking as much like it had been as possible. The barrels and their biochemical slurry were not disturbed. Not yet. Every entrance to the bank was put under surveillance, and the silent pursuit continued.

There were still loose threads that had to be followed, including two of the longest-running sets of payments that had been passing through the Haydon account. Money that the bank records showed had started up years previously when Suzanne Allen and her lodger mysteriously vanished from public life.

By this point, it was becoming increasingly apparent from the various witness statements that the connecting factor in the lives of so many of the identified victims was not Mark Haydon, but John Bunting. So when they discovered that he had lived on the same street as those two missing people, another warrant was sought to dig up the back garden of the property.

Just like the original burials, this excavation was carried out under the cover of darkness, in the dead of night when it seemed unlikely that any of Bunting's local friends might have their eyes on the place. When the two bodies were discovered, there was little surprise among the police. Not now that they knew what they were dealing with.

Unlike Snowtown, there was no way to secure this crime scene for forensic investigation without being obvious, so the police moved quickly.

John, Mark, Robert, and Jamie were arrested in a single swooping operation, securing each of the men first in their own home to ensure that they could not communicate with any of the others in the conspiracy, then transporting them all to the police station to be formally charged. They were not allowed to talk to each other. They were not allowed to get their stories straight. Not that even the most convincing of lies would have been sufficient, given the wealth of evidence against them.

John's confidence never faltered. He had been planning for this since the beginning. He had coached the others in what to say in this eventuality. They would get him on the fraud charges, there was no real getting around that. The records and the money were there, clear as day, but the murders? How were they going to pin a murder on him when there was no body? Back at the old property they'd find bones, but enough years had passed now that he was certain they'd need dental records to identify either one of them, and even with those records, there was no proof that he had anything to do with the killings. He hadn't even lived in that house for years. What did it have to do with him if there were bones in the garden? None of his people were going to testify that he'd put them there, were they?

As for the bodies in the vault, he knew his chemistry well enough that there would be nothing left of them. Sure, they might smell bad, and there might be traces of human matter inside the barrels, but that did not constitute a body. No body, no murder.

The media frenzy descended upon Snowtown, and the rural community suddenly came under so much public scrutiny that the local leadership had to beg the police to make a statement and get all of the reporters ruining the name of their town to back off. The most odious of the national newspaper reporters was spotted on his hands and knees outside the front door of the bank, sniffing to see if he could get a whiff of the corpses. It was intolerable. So the police came out and stated clearly that nobody from Snowtown was responsible for the crimes, that the murders did not even seem to have been committed there, and that the degenerate subculture behind the murders had chosen that place to store the bodies specifically because it was so quiet and harmless a place. Above suspicion.

It did little to help.

Time passed as the state did its due diligence, gathering up all of the evidence that could tie Bunting and his crew to the crimes, but John, in his isolated cell, remained convinced that he could walk away untouched, probably with time served. He barely even bothered to talk with his lawyers after issuing his initial instructions, and when he heard that the courts didn't even seem to be pursuing most of the fraud charges, he genuinely thought that he'd gotten away scot-free. He had always known that he was the smartest man in the room, but even he hadn't thought that he'd be able to stroll out without even a short sentence.

That arrogance would prove to be his undoing.

John's knowledge of chemistry remained entirely rooted in his high school education. He had not attended college, attended any advanced classes, or even studied the subject himself after those classes. He was so certain in his knowledge that he'd never even bothered to look up the chemical mixtures that he was using in the barrels. Why would he when he knew it all?

If he hadn't been so sure of himself, then he might have known that using an entirely different acid from the one that he was accustomed to working with in his science classes would have had an entirely different result in the concentrations that he was using. Instead of dissolving the bodies, he had pickled them. Perfectly preserving them at the moment of death.

The bodies in the ground had decayed to the point that almost all evidence of the torture was gone, but the ones in the barrels still showed every cut, burn and bruise. The full testament of John's crimes had been perfectly preserved. The coroner was able to pinpoint their time of death, method of death, and even the order of the tortures that they had been put through. John's arrogant certainty that he knew better than everyone else had doomed him.

With the coroner's reports, combined with the tools, chemicals, and ropes found in John's car, home, the bank, and the homes of the others involved, there was ample evidence against them. But it still wasn't enough to tie him to all of the murders that he was suspected of. Clinton Trezise and Thomas Trevilyan had both been discovered since their death, and their cases remained unsolved or misfiled as suicide, respectively. What the Australian justice system needed was an insider. Somebody who was a part of the cabal, willing to give evidence against it. At first, they thought that they had found that person in Jodie Elliot, who had lost her son and sister to the killers, but despite the fact that she was easy to lead into giving testimony, it soon became apparent that, despite her close proximity to the killers and victims, she was blissfully unaware of the majority of what was going on. She could attest to the fraud, as she was an accomplice in it, but the killings? No. She didn't know enough to be useful.

In the end, it was another death that brought John Bunting's campaign of terror to an end. One that even he couldn't take credit for.

James Vlassakis's mother, Elizabeth Harvey, had been suffering in silence with a slow-growing cancer for several years, and while he was awaiting trial in the same stalwart silence as the rest of them, it finally caught up to her. At first, he could not believe that she was dead. He thought that it was some kind of trick. But then the reality of the situation sank in.

Jamie had lost his last real connection to the outside world, but in isolation from John, he had also gained clarity. The manipulation that he had been experiencing for his entire adult life became steadily more clear to him, and remorse began to bite at him. Everyone that he had called family or friend had been lost to him, and it was all because of John. John had driven the wedge between him and everyone that he knew and loved. He had isolated Jamie so that he could use him for his own purposes. He had never raped him the way his birth father had, but he had changed him just as surely for the worse, inflicting trauma after trauma on him until he had felt like there was nobody in the world that could protect him. Nobody except for John.

The only person other than John who would be hurt by the truth was his mother, and now she was beyond any earthly harm. It was time for Jamie to start looking after himself.

He cut a deal with the prosecution. He would provide a full account of what the others had done, plead guilty to the crimes that he was involved in, and accept the sentences for them without complaint. He knew that there was already enough evidence against him to guarantee his imprisonment, so he didn't offer up his guilty pleas as a part of the deal. Rather he asked for something a little more clever.

Throughout the trial, and in the run-up to it, there had been numerous suppression orders handed down by the court to protect the identity of the perpetrators and the victims from the voracious media. All that Jamie wanted was for that anonymity to continue after his conviction. No photos of him. No physical descriptions of him. No courtroom artists. You will find that even the book in your hands right now contains no description of him that could be used to identify him, because those suppression orders are still in effect.

While the rest of the conspirators became famous, and a target for vengeance as the most prolific serial killers in Australia, Jamie was allowed to fade into the background. To change his name and serve out his sentences in relative peace, far from all the rest of the cabal. He denied none of his culpability, but he did not want to be tarred with the same brush as the others.

As things spiralled further and further out of John's control, he sank deeper and deeper into his fantasy. He was a crusader against the predators of the world, not the monster that the stuffed suits in court were trying to paint him as. But he'd have his day in court, he'd have his chance to stand up and tell the world what he had done. To stand up proudly and make his statement. Once and for all.

The first of them to reach court was Jamie, who pleaded guilty to the four murders that he was involved in, receiving a life sentence for each one, and departing court to begin serving them on the 21st of June, 2001.

John was tried alongside Robert Wagner, as the two involved in the most killings and most easily identified as the beneficiaries of the crimes. Mark Haydon's case was more complex, as he had not been directly involved in the majority of the murders, only appearing on the scene after the actual crimes had been completed. The three of them appeared together only once, to enter their plea of not guilty to ten of the killings. Despite the insurmountable evidence against them, John meant to make the justice system work if they wanted him caged. The court was forced to proceed with a trial by jury, something that proved more difficult than anyone could have anticipated. Jurors, too sickened and horrified by the evidence being presented, would drop out, triggering a restart to the trial each time. Three jurors in total were reported to have dropped out over the course of the trial, but there was no way for the press to know for certain as the suppression orders were still in full effect.

Finally, the time came for John to take to the stand, and he didn't even pretend that he wasn't going to implicate himself in all of the crimes. He didn't want to deny his involvement, he wanted to be applauded for it. He was the ringmaster of the circus, and he craved the applause of the audience. He stood up in court and proudly announced, 'There are paedophiles and predators out there, hurting your children, and the police do nothing. I did something. I stopped them.'

He may as well have signed a full confession. With all of the other evidence, including Jamie's testimony and recordings that the police had made using a device planted in Haydon's house during their investigation, there was no denying their involvement anymore. The jury convicted them on all counts, barring the death of Suzanne Allen, whose case it was decided there was insufficient evidence to pursue. John's story of discovering her body and merely benefitting from the death seemed to fit with what was known of his behaviour.

Together with Robert Wagner, John was convicted of ten murders on the eighth of September, 2003, and remanded to custody.

Haydon's trial was considerably more complex due to his limited involvement until after the fact. It recommenced in 2004, eventually culminating in his conviction on multiple counts of 'assisting offenders' but failing to pin any of the murders on him. There were also multiple counts that the jury could not reach a decision on, opening up the possibility of a retrial in the near future.

John and Robert pressed for appeals constantly, finally being rejected by the Supreme Court in May of 2005 with an official statement from the deciding judge that they were 'in the business of killing for pleasure' and 'incapable of true rehabilitation'.

Mark remained in a kind of legal limbo until he finally reached an agreement with the court in the run-up to his second trial, pleading guilty to two new charges of assisting in the murder of Troy Youde and his wife.

The final outstanding charge for the murder of Suzanne Allen was dropped once and for all in May 2007, when a jury was unable to decide whether she had been murdered or not.

Legal challenges continue, and it becomes more and more likely with each passing year that one or more of the killers will receive clemency from the court and be released on parole. The only one who most certainly will not walk the streets a free man again is, ironically, James Vlassakis. The only one who has shown anything even resembling remorse for his involvement in the crimes.

The slow and steady pace of the police's investigation was certainly a contributing factor to its success, but the death of David Johnson was also the inevitable result of their careful diligence. Yet long before David's death, another killing had been surely committed by the cabal.

Even today, the name of Snowtown is inexorably tied to the crimes that John Bunting and his cabal committed. For a time, it saw an influx of tourists as true crime enthusiasts passed through, but it did little to help with the stigma that afflicted the town in every other aspect and industry. In a way, Snowtown could be considered the last victim of Bunting's campaign of violence. And slowly but surely, it is dying as a result of his actions.

The cultural impact of Australia's most prolific serial killers cannot be fully measured, but even to this day, you barely have to scratch the surface before you find someone claiming that John Bunting was in the right. Someone who has heard his declaration of himself as an avenger of the abused and bought into that macho-man fantasy, entirely ignoring that the majority of his crimes were rooted in sadism, neo-Nazi ideology and personal gain.

Despite his evil being exposed to the world, there seems to remain the same simmering discontent just below the surface of polite society, a fresh degenerate subculture just waiting for an excuse to lash out at anyone who is different, labelling them as the abusers. The monsters.

It would be more comfortable for us to ascribe some magical power of manipulation to the sociopath. To picture John Bunting as a spider in human clothing, perched at the centre of his web of lies, pulling the strings of those around him like a puppet master. The truth is less fantastical, but considerably more upsetting. John was a talented manipulator who devoted no small part of his daily energies to controlling the emotional states and thoughts of those in his inner circle, but in this, he was not remarkable.

The world is full of men like John Bunting, and he had no special tools that he used to enact his will. The murders, the fraud, the conspiracy, all were built from tiny bricks of mundane evil. The neo-Nazi ideology that John had absorbed as a teenager allowed him to infect others who were vulnerable to its rhetoric.

The guilt and the fear of danger from the other conspirators was certainly a factor in their choice to remain silent throughout the years, but no more a factor than the steady flow of money that the group's fraudulent activities generated. Ultimately, all of the evil that was done in John's name was done by regular people who simply had nothing better to do with their lives. People who had been pushed so far to the periphery of civilisation that they no longer felt any benefit in upholding the most basic tenets of decency or the social contract.

Looking back on John Bunting's personal history, it is easy to see how he came to be vulnerable to the ideologies of hate. He suffered a grotesque and terrible trauma at a young and formative age. An event that changed his whole perspective on the world and can easily be tracked through to the choices that he later made. Yet there are millions of other children who suffer equally terrible events without growing up to become mass murderers, and it is a gross disservice to them to claim that trauma makes monsters out of men.

John chose to embrace hatred. He chose to pursue his vendetta against all gay men, because they were a socially acceptable target, and then against anyone whom he felt might pose opposition to him. He decided, day after day, that his comfort was worth more than the lives of those he slaughtered so that he might reap the rewards of their benefits money. He chose to do evil.

Nowhere could that have been more clear than in the rooms where he chose to murder. There was no reason to torture any one of his victims if the money, or simply their extermination from the world, was his goal. He did that because he enjoyed it. He enjoyed hurting people. That was not the result of his trauma or early indoctrination into neo-Nazi ideology or anything else. That was John choosing for his pleasure at the cost of someone else's pain. And he went on choosing it. He chose to do evil at every single opportunity. To kill innocent people, to kill his co-conspirators, to murder friends and family, women and children.

All were fair game for John, and even to him, his campaign against paedophilia must have seemed a pretty flimsy excuse by the end.

To say that John Bunting was a sociopath – divorced from his humanity and therefore none of our concern – is to deny the truth. Bunting never showed any of the traditional signs of sociopathy. Indeed, if he had no sense of empathy, then he would have been far less adept at social manipulation. John Bunting knew that what he was doing was wrong, and he chose to do it anyway. He knew the pain that his victims were suffering, but he elected for it to happen all the same. He was a normal man who chose to change his trajectory from upwardly mobile to a deep delve into the pits of depravity because he enjoyed it down there.

Want More?

Did you enjoy *No Place For The Weak* and want some more True Crime?

YOUR FREE BOOK IS WAITING

From bestselling author Ryan Green

There is a man who is officially classed as "**Britain's most dangerous prisoner**"

The man's name is Robert Maudsley, and his crimes earned him the nickname "**Hannibal the Cannibal**"

This free book is an exploration of his story...

★★★★★ *"Ryan brings the horrifying details to life. I can't wait to read more by this author!"*

Get a free copy of ***Robert Maudsley: Hannibal the Cannibal*** when you sign up to join my Reader's Group.

www.ryangreenbooks.com/free-book

Every Review Helps

If you enjoyed the book and have a moment to spare, I would really appreciate a short review on Amazon. Your help in spreading the word is gratefully received and reviews make a huge difference to helping new readers find me. Without reviewers, us self-published authors would have a hard time!

Type in your link below to be taken straight to my book review page.

US	geni.us/noplaceUS
UK	geni.us/noplaceUK
Australia	geni.us/noplaceAUS
Canada	geni.us/noplaceCA

Thank you! I can't wait to read your thoughts.

About Ryan Green

Ryan Green is a true crime author who lives in Herefordshire, England with his wife, three children, and two dogs. Outside of writing and spending time with his family, Ryan enjoys walking, reading and windsurfing.

Ryan is fascinated with History, Psychology and True Crime. In 2015, he finally started researching and writing his own work and at the end of the year, he released his first book on Britain's most notorious serial killer, Harold Shipman.

He has since written several books on lesser-known subjects, and taken the unique approach of writing from the killer's perspective. He narrates some of the most chilling scenes you'll encounter in the True Crime genre.

You can sign up to Ryan's newsletter to receive a free book, updates, and the latest releases at:

WWW.RYANGREENBOOKS.COM

More Books by Ryan Green

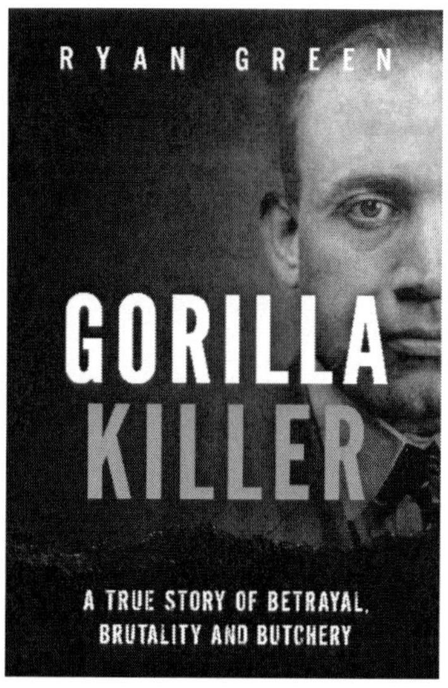

On 20th February 1926, landlady Clara Newman (60) opened her door to a potential tenant who enquired into the availability of one of her rooms. Despite his grim and bulky appearance, he introduced himself politely, in a soft-spoken voice whilst clutching a Bible in one of his large hands. She invited him in. The moment he stepped into her home, he lunged forwards, wrapping his over-sized fingers around her throat and forced her to the ground. She couldn't scream. He had learned the dangers of a scream. She slowly slipped into darkness. Given what would follow, it was probably a kindness.

The 'Gorilla Killer', Earle Nelson, roamed over 7,000 miles of North America undetected, whilst satisfying his deranged desires. During a span of almost two years, he choked the life out of more than twenty unsuspecting women, subjected their bodies to the most unspeakable acts, and seemingly enjoyed the process.

More Books by Ryan Green

On 23 January 1978, David Wallin returned to an unlit home. His pregnant wife, Teresa (22), was nowhere to be seen. The radio was still playing and there were some peculiar stains on the carpet. Wallin nervously followed the stains to his bedroom and encountered a scene so chilling that it would haunt him for the rest of his life. Teresa had been sexually assaulted and mutilated. She was also missing body parts and large volumes of blood.

Four days later, the Sacramento Police Department were called to a home approximately a mile away from the Wallin residence. They were not prepared for the horror that awaited them. Daniel Meredith (56) and Jason Miroth (6) were shot multiple times. Evelyn Miroth (38) was disfigured, disembowelled and abused like Teresa. She was also missing body parts and large quantities of blood. David Ferreira (2), who Evelyn was babysitting, was nowhere to be seen and likely in the hands of the deranged mass murderer.

More Books by Ryan Green

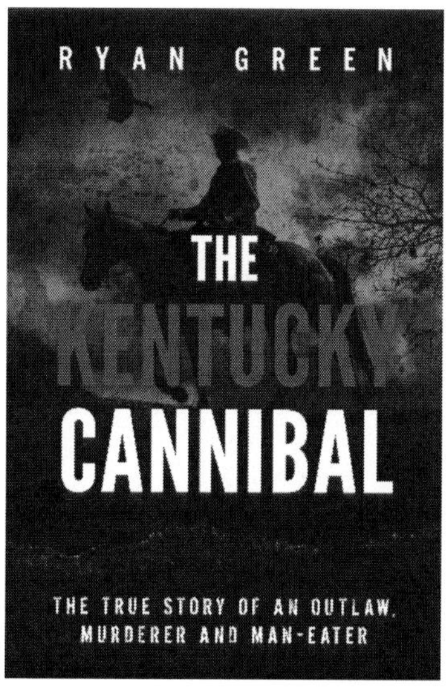

In 1850, following a divorce and a number of encounters with the law, Boone Helm headed 'Out West' to chase the Californian Gold Rush with his cousin. When his cousin pulled out at the last minute, Helm was incensed, and brutally stabbed him to death. Helm was detained in an asylum for the mentally disturbed but managed to escape.

Helm continued his journey west with renewed vigour, where he opportunistically killed and consumed the flesh of adversaries and travelling companions, earning him the nickname 'The Kentucky Cannibal'. After several brutal months in the wilderness, he finally made it California. At a time where violence was the law of the land, Helm's savage set of skills could finally be recognised and rewarded.

More Books by Ryan Green

In 1974, the US East Coast was whipped up into a frenzy of fear. Locking their windows and doors, everyone was terrified of becoming the next victim of the strikingly handsome but deadly "*Casanova Killer*". And he was on the move.

After being released from jail and promptly abandoned by his fiancée, Paul John Knowles embarked on a spate of gruesome murders on a road trip up the Pacific Coast.

No room for fear, no room for guilt, just the road

As the man-hunt gathered pace, the cold-blooded killing spree continued to defy detectives. With no visible pattern in the age, race nor gender of the victims, Knowle's joyride of kidnap, rape and murder tore across multiple state borders. It became a race of tragically high stakes. How many more lives would be lost before the police finally caught up.

Free True Crime Audiobook

Sign up to Audible and use your free credit to download this collection of twelve books. If you cancel within 30 days, there's no charge!

WWW.RYANGREENBOOKS.COM/FREE-AUDIOBOOK

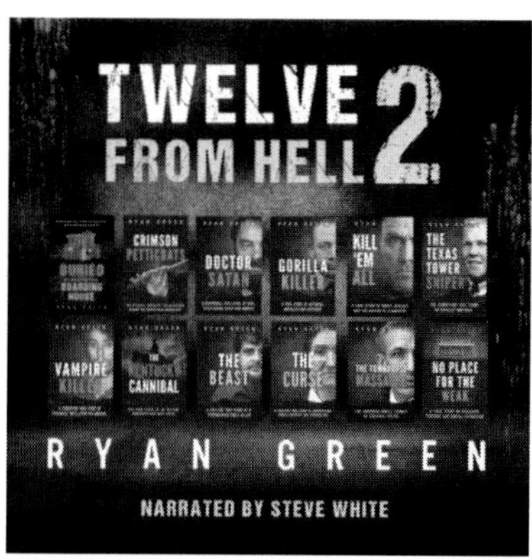

"Ryan Green has produced another excellent book and belongs at the top with true crime writers such as M. William Phelps, Gregg Olsen and Ann Rule" –**B.S. Reid**

"Wow! Chilling, shocking and totally riveting! I'm not going to sleep well after listening to this but the narration was fantastic. Crazy story but highly recommend for any true crime lover!" –**Mandy**

"Torture Mom by Ryan Green left me pretty speechless. The fact that it's a true story is just...wow" –**JStep**

"Graphic, upsetting, but superbly read and written" –**Ray C**

WWW.RYANGREENBOOKS.COM/FREE-AUDIOBOOK

Made in United States
North Haven, CT
25 June 2024

54058899R00081